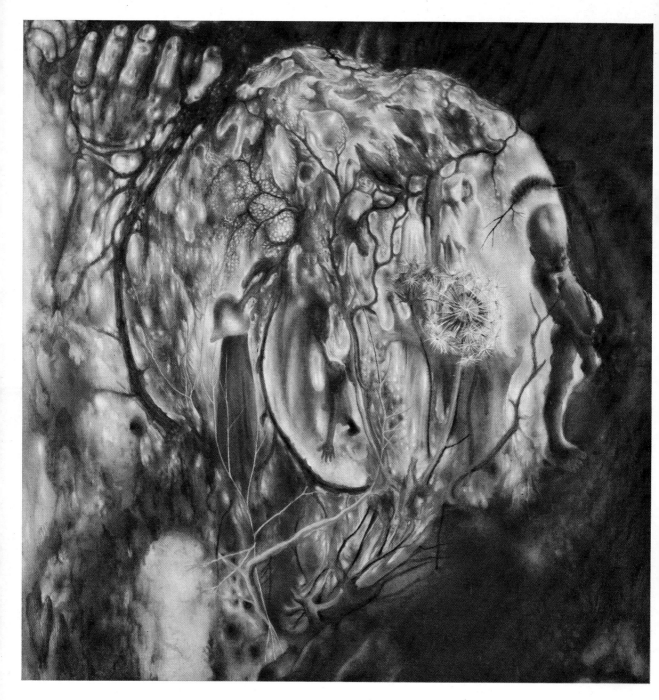

Hide-and-Seek, 1940-42. (Detail: "Head of Spring.") The Museum of Modern Art, New York, Mrs. Simon Guggenheim Fund. (See page 87 for complete picture.)

TCHELITCHEW

paintings · drawings

y james thrall soby

museum of modern art, new york

CONTENTS

ACKNOWLEDGMENTS

I want first of all to thank the artist for his generous and patient collaboration and for supplying me with copious notes which Mr. Parker Tyler was kind enough to transcribe.

The bibliography and list of previous exhibitions are largely the painstaking work of Mr. Bernard Karpel, Acting Librarian of the Museum of Modern Art.

I wish also to express appreciation to the following for the assistance they have given in assembling the exhibition and preparing the catalog: R. Kirk Askew, Jr.; Alfred H. Barr, Jr.; Professor Ralph W. Church; Sir Kenneth Clark; Henry Clifford; Charles Henri Ford; Geoffrey Gorer; Miss Eleanor Howland; Edward James; Mr. and Mrs. Sherman Kent; George Platt Lynes; Russell Lynes; Dr. Arthur Michel; Frank Perls; Daniel Catton Rich; Miss Agnes Rindge; Paul Schweikher; Monroe Wheeler.

JAMES THRALL SOBY
Director of the Exhibition

Lenders to the Exhibition

Mr. and Mrs. John E. Abbott, New York; Dr. Robert H. Alexander, New York; Mr. and Mrs. R. Kirk Askew, Jr., New York; A. Everett Austin, Jr., Hartford, Connecticut; Mrs. Le Ray Berdeau, New York; Harry A. Bull, New York; Mrs. E. Gerry Chadwick, New York; Professor Ralph W. Church, Santa Barbara, California; Mr. and Mrs. Henry Clifford, Radnor, Pennsylvania; Mr. and Mrs. Paul W. Cooley, West Hartford, Connecticut; Dr. Burrill B. Crohn, New York; Bernard Davis, Philadelphia; Miss Lucy Martin Donnelly, Bryn Mawr, Pennsylvania; Mrs. Thomas Hart Fisher, Chicago; Charles Henri Ford, New York; Dr. A. L. Garbat, New York; Mrs. Charles B. Goodspeed, Chicago; Edward James, South Laguna, California; Mrs. Oliver B. Jennings, New York; Julien Levy Gallery, New York; Edgar Kaufmann, Pittsburgh; Mr. and Mrs. Sherman Kent, Washington, D. C.; Lincoln Kirstein, New York; Leon Kochnitzky, New York; Mr. and Mrs. John La Touche, New York; Julien Levy, New York; Mrs. Joseph Louchheim, Washington, D. C.; Wright Ludington, Santa Barbara, California; George Platt Lynes, New York; Mr. and Mrs. Russell Lynes, Bryn Mawr, Pennsylvania; Mrs. Josiah P. Marvel, Princeton, New Jersey; Museum of Fine Arts, Boston; Allen Porter, New York; Miss Margaret C. Prall, Berkeley, California; Miss Helen Resor, New York; Lieut. Stanley R. Resor, New York; Miss Agnes Rindge, Poughkeepsie, New York; Mrs. Francis Robbins, Jr., New York; Mme. Helena Rubinstein, New York; Mrs. Charles H. Russell, Jr., New York; Mr. and Mrs. James Thrall Soby, Farmington, Connecticut; Maurice J. Speiser, New York; James Johnson Sweeney, New York; Pavel Tchelitchew, New York; Raimund von Hofmannstahl, New York; Wadsworth Atheneum, Hartford, Connecticut; Miss Edith Wetmore, New York; Monroe Wheeler, New York; Mr. and Mrs. John C. Wilson, New York; Mr. and Mrs. Howard Woolf, Scarsdale, New York.

Staff of the Museum

Alfred H. Barr, Jr., *Director;* John E. Abbott, *Executive Vice-President;* Monroe Wheeler, *Director of Exhibitions and Publications;* Frances Hawkins, *Secretary;* Ione Ulrich, *Assistant Treasurer and Comptroller.*

Department of Painting and Sculpture: Alfred H. Barr, Jr., *Curator;* Dorothy C. Miller, *Associate Curator;* Elise Van Hook, *Assistant.*

Department of Architecture: Alice M. Carson, *Acting Curator.*

Film Library: John E. Abbott, *Director;* Iris Barry, *Curator;* Edward F. Kerns, *Technical Director;* Allen Porter, *Circulation and Exhibition Director* *.

Department of Industrial Design: Eliot F. Noyes, *Director* *; Alice M. Carson, *Acting Director.*

Department of Photography: Beaumont Newhall, *Curator* *; Nancy Newhall, *Assistant in Charge.*

Department of Exhibitions: Monroe Wheeler, *Director;* Carlos Dyer, *Technical Assistant.*

Department of Circulating Exhibitions: Elodie Courter, *Director.*

Department of Publications: Monroe Wheeler, *Director;* Holger E. Hagen, *Manager* *; Frances Pernas, *Assistant Manager.*

Library: Beaumont Newhall, *Librarian* *; Bernard Karpel, *Acting Librarian.*

Dance Archives: Paul Magriel, *Librarian* *; Sidney Edison, *Acting Librarian.*

Publicity Department: Sarah Newmeyer, *Director.*

Department of Registration: Dorothy H. Dudley, *Registrar.*

Educational Project: Victor D'Amico, *Director.*

Armed Services Program: James Thrall Soby, *Director.*

Production Manager: Rand Warren.

Information Desk: Lillian W. Clark.

* On leave of absence with the armed services.

BRIEF CHRONOLOGY

1898   Pavel Tchelitchew born in Moscow, Russia, September 21.

Early youth   Made numerous drawings, influenced by macabre romanticism of book illustrations by Gustave Doré and Vrubel. Education acquired privately and in local schools.

1918–20   Fled Soviet Revolution with family, arriving in Kiev in the fall of 1918. Attended classes in drawing at Kiev Academy. Encouraged by Alexandra Exter, a pupil of Fernand Léger. Given private instruction in painting by Basil Tchakrigine and Isaac Rabinovitch. Worked on theatre projects and posters as apprentice to local abstract artists.

1920–21   Traveled in the Levant: Constantinople, Sofia.

1921–23   Lived and worked in Berlin. Executed stage designs for a cabaret-music hall, for ballets, the legitimate theatre and the Berlin State Opera.

1923   Moved to Paris. Painted landscapes and portraits. Reacted against abstract art.

1925   Showed in *Salon d'Automne*.

1926   Took part in exhibition of group of painters afterwards called "Neo-Romantics" at Galerie Druet, Feb. 22-Mar. 5.

1925–27   Evolved "laconic" compositions. First painted multiple images in *The Ship* (1926). Visits to South of France and Algiers brought him to use of blue as predominant color. Used composite technique—sand and coffee mixed with gouache. Earliest circus pictures, 1927.

1928–29   Commenced to use violent distortions of perspective, 1928. Painted figure pieces composed of interior, metamorphic imagery.

First one-man exhibition, Claridge Gallery, London, July, 1928. Second one-man exhibition, Galerie Pierre, Paris, June, 1929.

Designed scenery and costumes for the ballet, *Ode*, produced by Diaghilev, 1928.

1930–31   Wine red often replaced blue as predominant color in an almost monochromatic palette.

Still-life figures, 1930. "Spahi" and "The Loges" series, 1931.

1932–33   Tattooed figures; final years of circus theme. Used brighter and more contrasting colors.

Designed scenery and costumes for the ballet, *L'Errante*, 1933.

1934   "Tennis players" series. Visit to Spain. "Bullfight" series. Beginning of use of triple perspective.

Arrived in America, October, 1934. First one-man exhibition in this country, Julien Levy Gallery, New York.

1935   First trip to Italy. Conceived composition of *Phenomena*, and painted many preliminary oils and gouaches for it.

1936   Decorated Avery Memorial Museum (The Wadsworth Atheneum, Hartford), for Paper Ball, February.

Designed scenery and costumes for the ballets, *Magic* and *Orpheus*.

1937–38   Worked on *Phenomena*, completed spring 1938. Painted many portraits and made numerous silverpoint drawings.

Designed scenery and costumes for the ballet, *St. Francis*, 1938.

1938–40   Lived for most part in Weston, Connecticut. Deeply moved by autumn foliage. Interest in metamorphic forms revived by resemblance of leaves to children in cloaks. Adopted brilliant, "autumn" palette.

Returned to France for brief visit, 1939. Designed scenery and costumes for the play, *Ondine*.

1940–42   Spent summers of 1940 and 1941 at Derby Hill, Vermont. Made many metamorphic landscape drawings and a few paintings. Automatism played important part in their inspiration.

Moved to New York City 1941, has lived there since. In 1941 designed scenery and costumes for the ballets, *Balustrade* and *Cave of Sleep* (unproduced).

June, 1942, designed scenery and costumes for the ballet, *Apollon Musagète*, and for a second ballet, *Concerto*, to Mozart's music.

July, 1942, completed *Hide-and-Seek*, begun summer of 1940.

PAVEL TCHELITCHEW

Childhood in Russia. Kiev (1918–20).

PAVEL TCHELITCHEW was born in Moscow on September 21, 1898. His family belonged to the aristocracy and his education was largely acquired through private tutors. He read a great deal in the family library where he found and was deeply impressed by books illustrated by Gustave Doré and the Polish illustrator, Vrubel. His instinctive taste for the fantastic was evident in the drawings he made as a child, and at the age of eight after having painted an oil portrait of his mother he completed a *Head of Medusa* inspired by Doré's turgid romanticism.

For a time he was undecided whether to become an artist or a dancer, a dilemma which was settled for him by his father's insistence that he promise never to dance professionally. Even without his father's unequivocal word on the subject, Tchelitchew would certainly have arrived at his own decision to become a painter. As he grew older he made more and more drawings, forcing his hand to acquire the technical skill necessary to transcribe an imagination inflamed by fairy tales, stories of adventure and Doré's images. He pored over his family's volumes on the stage designs of Bakst and Benois, but he also looked carefully at monographs on the great European masters of painting. His nurse and he often played a game of cards in which scoring was based on ability to identify masterpieces of art engraved on the backs of the cards. By this admirable method he grew to love the works of Botticelli, Raphael, Tintoretto and Rembrandt. He came to loathe the art of Rubens, a distaste which was partly natural and partly the result of an impatience with the number of Rubens's compositions which turned up during the course of the card game.

When the Revolution came the Tchelitchew family might have escaped the Soviet wrath if they had been judged on political grounds alone, since the elder Tchelitchew was known as a liberal who had long since urged the distribution of land rights to the peasants. But they were listed with their class, and in the fall of 1918 they fled Moscow for Kiev where Tchelitchew's older sister and her husband had a large estate. Food in Kiev was scarce, even unobtainable for thousands, but the city was faring better than most in Russia and had therefore attracted a number of the leading Russian artists. Tchelitchew was twenty and determined, with his family's blessing, to become a professional painter. Through Pierre Suvitchinsky, a patron of the arts, he soon met Alexandra Exter, who conducted a school for painters and stage designers to whom she imparted the devotion to abstract art that she had herself acquired in Paris under the tutelage of Fernand Léger. Mme. Exter befriended the young artist and it may have been she who inspired in him the belief, so inevitable for the generation of Diaghilev and so persistent in Russia, that the theatre offers a major field rather than a minor diversion for the easel painter's talents. If so, our debt to her must be extravagantly measured, since Tchelitchew has plainly become one of the few great stage designers of his period.

In Kiev as elsewhere in Russia the tradition of abstract art, springing from Parisian Cubism, had received new impetus from the researches of Malevich and the native Constructivists.* (This was the period before the Soviet Government had decided to convert contemporary art to its own propaganda purpose, and abstract painting was still considered a proper vehicle for revolutionary fervor.) The leading local painter in Kiev, Bogomazov, was a Cubist and the doctrine of abstraction completely dominated the group of anti-academic artists whose company Tchelitchew immediately joined. The Kiev Academy held a number of "free" courses in which for a nominal fee artists were allowed to work from the model without benefit of formal instruction. Tchelitchew attended these courses but profited more from private lessons given him by Isaac Rabinovitch, now one of the most famous theatre designers in Soviet Russia, and Basil Tchakrigine. Both of these men were working in the Cubist-Constructivist direction and Tchelitchew assisted them in various projects. He helped Rabinovitch execute the sets and costumes for a small music hall having weekly changes of program, and he worked under Bogomazov on posters for numerous festivals held in Kiev. Presently he met such important figures in the ballet as Mme. Nijinska and Mordkin but worked on no stage décors of his own until he was asked by a leading producer, Mardganov, to design a dramatic production. The advance of the White Army on Kiev cancelled the project in its preliminary phase.

Tchelitchew's style was at this time completely abstract, with strong overtones of Léger's pre-war manner and of native Constructivism. By 1919, however, he began to show signs of independence from Rabinovitch, Tchakrigine and his other companions. For these men the cone and rectangle still held the sacrosanct status imposed by the Cubists, but Tchelitchew gradually found that these rigid forms constrained his imagination. His painting became slightly more representational and he evolved the theory that a line cannot be straight because it must have an end and be related to man's spherical existence. The theory is an interesting forecast both of Tchelitchew's continuing regard for the implications of the cosmic and of his present curvilinear exuberance of style.

Travel in the Levant. Berlin (1921–23).

In the winter of 1919 Tchelitchew completed his first big canvas, a portrait of Mme. Paul Kochansky. During the autumn of 1920 he left Kiev for Odessa where he designed several minor music hall productions for a pupil of Mordkin, making the costumes and painting the

---

* "Constructivism: A movement related technically and esthetically to architecture and engineering as much as to sculpture. It began about 1914 in Russia under the influence of Parisian Cubism, and later spread throughout Europe and America. Constructions are often built of metal, celluloid or glass and are usually abstract in design. . . ." Alfred H. Barr, Jr., *Painting and Sculpture in the Museum of Modern Art.*

sets himself. He executed numerous drawings in which the contours of his subjects were defined by the linked, semi-circular lines to which his reaction against straight lines had led him. Living in desperate poverty, he moved on to Constantinople and then to Sofia. He arrived in Berlin in the autumn of 1921 and stayed there until 1923 when he went to Paris to live.

Perhaps as a relief from the all too prophetic commiseration of the German Expressionists, Berlin patrons of art and the theatre were taking a passionate interest in the work of Central European and Russian abstractionists and Tchelitchew was soon given a series of commissions for stage décors and costumes. For *Der Blaue Vogel* (The Blue Bird Theatre), a cabaret-type of music hall, he executed sets and costumes on the following themes: a Dutch number, with costumes made of burlap bags soaked in house paint; a scene in a Russian monastery; a number based on popular cartoons; a Chinese love story; a Spanish number; a Russian wedding feast; and a production of *Le roi fait battre le tambour*. The first of these programs was produced October 5, 1922.

The *Russisches Romantisches Theater* (Russian Romantic Theatre) was inaugurated in the Apollo Theatre, Berlin, in the summer of 1922 and Tchelitchew did the sets and costumes for two of its most ambitious productions. These were *Bojarenhochzeit* (produced October 14, 1922), a "dance painting" conceived by the theatre's choreographer, Boris Romanov; and *Tempelopfer der Atoraga* (produced January 24, 1923), with choreography by Romanov and Glazunov's music. A principal dancer in both productions was Claudia Pavlova, of whom Tchelitchew was to paint two portraits in Paris in 1925. The successful completion of these two commissions led to his being asked to design the décor and costumes for an important production of the play, *Savonarola*, derived from the Gobineau chronicles and presented at the *Theater in der Königgrätzerstrasse* in 1923. The Berlin State Opera commissioned him to do the sets and costumes for the Rimski-Korsakov opera, *Coq d'Or*, also produced in 1923.

Tchelitchew's work in Berlin appears to have been enthusiastically received and is said to have widely influenced German stage designers during the mid-1920's. Unfortunately documentation on his productions is extremely limited. To judge by the few photographs still in the artist's possession, the influence of Léger and the Russian Constructivists was still strongly felt in both costumes and sets. *Savonarola* was the most Constructivist of all his productions and it is significant that during his years in Berlin Tchelitchew was friendly with one of the leading Constructivists, Lissitzky, then living in the German capital. A more detailed analysis of Tchelitchew's early period in the theatre must await the study of his entire career as a stage designer which some day, surely, will be published. Meanwhile there is one point—a strangely neglected point—which can be discussed with some certainty from the evidence at hand: the influence of the painter's Cubist-Constructivist period on his own later development as an artist.

The most tangible clue to this influence is provided by the few relatively abstract compositions which Tchelitchew executed in France in 1926, an outstanding example being *The Ship* (plate 8). The medium of these pictures—sand and coffee mixed with roof paint or gouache—was suggested to the artist by the former Cubist, Juan Gris, and Tchelitchew's

11

handling of the medium was probably affected by his regard for the rich texture of Georges Braque's compositions, which he preferred to those of Picasso. The wires strung across *The Ship* on matches embedded in the pigment seem Constructivist in derivation, though put to original use.

A further reflection of Constructivism is felt, however weakly, in certain of the painter's drawings for the 1928 ballet, *Ode* (nos. 196 and 197).* The figures in these drawings are related to each other by ropes which on the stage were carried about by the dancers. The function of the ropes could, of course, have been purely romantic-decorative, yet they appear to have been used primarily for structural effect. And even after Tchelitchew had abandoned the mechanical devices of *The Ship* and *Ode* for more painterly methods, he often retained something of their spatial function, as may be seen by comparing the wires of *The Ship* with the surface lines of *The Thinker* (plate 10) or the tightropes which appear in *Madame Bonjean* (plate 29).

The painter's abiding concern with sculptural depth and plasticity probably stems partially at least from his early career as a Constructivist. His connection with the Cubist-Constructivist tradition has been obscured in recent years by the violence of his humanist reaction against the abstract, the mechanical and the indecipherable. Obvious signs of the connection have become increasingly difficult to find, yet vestiges of the relationship may be more important than is commonly supposed. For instance it is probable that Tchelitchew's reverence for commonplace materials—his use of old newspapers to decorate the Wadsworth Atheneum's Paper Ball in 1936 (bibl. 20) is an extreme example—is inherited as much from the Picasso-Constructivist procedure as from the painter's own experience during the starvation years immediately after the war, when sets and costumes were made from the cheapest materials or were not made at all. His sense of composition owes much, as he is the first to insist, to abstract art and to this movement's great predecessor, Seurat. And most important of all, Tchelitchew's intellectuality, his ambition to violate appearances to their very core in order to arrive at a revolutionary formal reconstruction, relates him more closely in certain ways to the abstractionists' premise than to the Surrealists' anti-Reason or the scholasticism of the Neo-Romantic painters. The effect of his own early career and enthusiasms on his more recent work can easily be exaggerated, but it should not be ignored.

Arrival in Paris. Early Works. The "Salon d'Automne" of 1925.

During the last year of his stay in Berlin, Tchelitchew met Diaghilev and was asked by the great impresario to go to Paris to execute a commission for the ballet. The commission did not materialize until five years later, but in July, 1923, the painter arrived in the French capital. Almost at once he began to renounce the machine forms of Constructivism, though his

* As distinguished from plate references, this and all similar numbers refer to the catalog of the exhibition, p. 91, ff.

interest in them revived several years later, as noted above. He spent the autumn and early winter of 1924 painting landscapes in the Bois de Boulogne and in parts of Brittany, working for the most part with pastels and crayons. Gradually the human face began to fascinate him above all other subjects. In late 1924 and 1925 he finished several self-portraits and a number of portraits of friends with whom his psychological and emotional accord was intimate and continuous (e.g. plate 2). The earliest of these portraits—among them those of Mrs. George Antheil, Nicolas Nabokov, Glenway Wescott, Martha Dennison, Margaret Anderson, Bernadine Szold and her daughter Rosemary, Allen Tanner and Liudmila Belozvetov—were done in a very high key and according to the artist their baby blues and magenta pinks shocked even his friends. In a similar vein he painted figure pieces of dance hall girls, prostitutes (plate 1) and soldiers and sailors in faded blue uniforms. In the painter's words, "This subject matter of the tragic, macabre and lascivious remained for some time in my work." *

To the *Salon d'Automne* of 1925 Tchelitchew sent a portrait and also the *Basket of Strawberries* (plate 3), a picture which marked a turning point in his career. It was, to begin with, perhaps the first painting which extended his reputation as an easel painter beyond the circle of talented friends whom he had attracted since his arrival from Berlin. When shown in the Salon the canvas was singled out by several widely read critics, among them Florent Fels, who declared in *L'Art Vivant* (October 1, 1925) that Tchelitchew's gift was "indisputable" and added in summary: "A little still life representing a basket of strawberries forces us to note the name of Tchelitchew, still seldom heard." No less a collector than Miss Gertrude Stein left the Salon to inquire the artist's address and enthusiastically acclaimed his work (bibl. 33). Afterwards she took him to see her magnificent collection of Picassos. At Alfred Flechtheim's gallery in Berlin and in Parisian galleries and collections Tchelitchew had already seen innumerable Picassos, but they had been mostly of the Cubist and later periods. At Miss Stein's he saw the Rose period pictures of 1905–06 which were to have so vital an influence on his own paintings of 1929–32. His favorites were and remain *Woman with a Fan* (now in the collection of Mrs. William Averell Harriman, New York) and *Portrait of Gertrude Stein*.

Considered for its own sake, the *Basket of Strawberries* is possibly the first painting by Tchelitchew in which he approached maturity of style. The picture is painted in the lurid pink and rose which he had previously used in his brothel scenes and portraits. But in its narrow scale of tone and color it forecasts the close harmonies of *Madame Bonjean, Théâtre français* (plate 33) and other canvases of the early 1930's. Moreover, the angle from which the still life is viewed, though not uncommon in work by older artists of the period, reveals what was to become one of Tchelitchew's primary concerns: to wrench space from its normal context and extend the spatial limits imposed by average vision. The slant of the table is steepened more than that of the basket. The basket and its handle are projected into the picture space through a Gothic angularity of form which persisted in certain of Tchelitchew's figure pieces of 1926–28 (plate 7) and did not entirely disappear until Picasso's round, Rose period contours led Tchelitchew to his own clown series of 1929–32.

* This and all subsequent quotations by the artist are taken from notes supplied the writer by Tchelitchew.

The Subdued Palette. Neo-Romanticism at the Galerie Druet, 1926.

Whether or not Tchelitchew was impressed by general criticism of his gaudy colors, during the summer of 1925 he decided to revise his palette completely and, in his words, "threw away all but black, white, ochre, natural and burnt umber." In this low key he executed several gray and white still lifes of eggs (plate 5), the eggs usually numbering three, a number for which—with its multiples—the painter has a deep awe. (His interest in numerology recalls that of an earlier romantic artist, Caspar David Friedrich.) A few months later he returned to portraiture, again painting his friends Allen Tanner and Liudmila Belozvetov and adding a portrait of Catherine de Villier, ballerina of the Moscow Grand Opera and later of Diaghilev's company. These portraits retained the savage distortion of facial features which had characterized his pink and blue portraits of the previous year. In them are unmistakable signs of the expressionist tradition of portraiture which had been developing in Europe since the turn of the century, in Germany through Expressionism itself, in Paris through the impact of the Fauves, African sculpture, Picasso's experiments and the independent researches of men like Rouault, Soutine and Modigliani. But within the hard, arbitrary contours of Tchelitchew's portraits there is an implication of tender brooding and reverie which the portraiture of his elders for the most part lacked. By comparison with the latter, Tchelitchew's portraits are romantic or, as the term came to be, Neo-Romantic.

In the winter of 1926 the Galerie Druet, Paris, held a group exhibition from which sprang Neo-Romanticism as a formal and recognizable movement. Tchelitchew, Christian Bérard, Eugène Berman and his older brother Léonide, Kristians Tonny, J.-F. Laglenne, Pierre Charbonnier, L. de Angelis and Thérèse Debains were represented in the exhibition. However disparate their talents and ambitions, they were allied in a faith that art must return to its ancient concern with man and his emotions; all were intent upon restoring mystery, sentiment and that response to the mood of time and place which the Cubists had deliberately stifled. They represented, as the writer has pointed out elsewhere, the naturalist side of a romantic revival for which the Surrealists were providing a somnambulist complement. Tchelitchew was for a time considered their *chef d'école*, being the most experienced painter, but close association among artists of the group was of short duration. As was natural to original painters, each was basically different from the others. Tchelitchew was distinguished from his fellows by a more restless and probing intellectuality. In consequence his work falls into more sharply defined cycles than theirs. By comparison with their more gradual evolution, his progress has been marked at intervals by program and counter-program, though he has always held to a central direction and often turned back to call up the impetus of previous experience. It is this quality of revolution within himself which gives his painting in its best phases its freshness and vitality. His capacity for renewing his approach through theoretical seeking, whether cerebral or superstitious in nature, is most vividly illustrated by his recent painting, *Hide-and-Seek* (plate 68), but signs of it are evident as early as 1925.

14

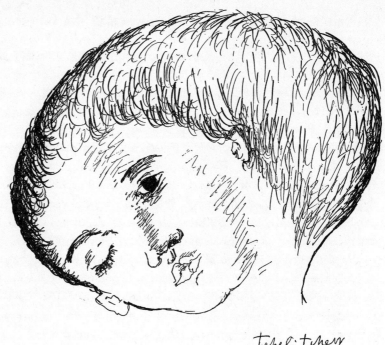

Asymmetrical Head, 1925.
Ink, 9 x 12⅛″. Collection
George Platt Lynes, New
York.

Tcheli·tchew

Simultaneous Aspects of a Single Image. "Laconic" Compositions (1925–27).

In the fall of 1925 Tchelitchew had attempted his own solution of a problem which had en-
grossed abstract painters of the older generation, particularly Picasso, and which has supplied
one of the most persistent themes in 20th century painting: the simultaneous presentation of
several different aspects of the human head and figure. He had really begun the attempt with
his still lifes of eggs executed during the summer, and had then turned these eggs into ovoid
human heads combined in various ways to portray the face in double profile and full-face (plate
4). At the same time he had experimented with cranial distortions as a means of providing a
framework for a double face, a procedure he had already approached in an oil nude of 1924–
25, *Mlle. Rose*, and in drawings of that period such as *Asymmetrical Head* (above). It was
symptomatic of Tchelitchew's new anti-abstractionism that he had retained in these images a
higher degree of representation and even characterization than Picasso and his followers had
thought necessary. Moreover, it is interesting that his ultimate solution of the problem should
have been found in subjects which nature had already multiplied in feature and form—the
freaks of *Phenomena* (plate 53). His conscience was on the side of psychological interpretation
rather than abstract design, and in his portrait of René Crevel painted late in 1925 (collection
Miss Gertrude Stein, Paris) he had shown three highly recognizable aspects of the poet's
head—from behind, in profile and full-face—by presenting them in successive planes, using a
minimum of distortion except in the common line of the hair which serves for two of the

15

The Mask, 1926. Ink. Collection the artist, Paris. *Not included in exhibition.*

Laconic Composition, 1926. Ink, 13⅞ x 9½". Julien Levy Gallery, New York.

heads. Some years later Salvador Dali was to adopt the latter device in double portraits of himself and his wife.

Early in 1926 Tchelitchew extended his experiments with simultaneity to include the human figure as well as the head. Possibly the first step in this direction is represented by drawings of that year in which the figure is handled as a single image while two aspects of the head are suggested by the ingenious expedient of showing the subject in the act of peeling off a mask. His use of this device became increasingly complex and resourceful (above left). Soon, however, he began to shift emphasis from the head to the figure. A single representational image of the head was retained and other aspects were symbolized by blank oval forms, a solution to which he may have been led equally by his own still lifes of eggs and by de Chirico's featureless mannequins of 1915, shown at the Galerie Paul Guillaume in Paris in June, 1926. At first Tchelitchew's figures were combined in a single image as seen from two angles, as in the *Nude in Space* (plate 6). Finally he evolved what he called the system of "laconic" composition. The development reached its climax in the *Portrait of Jacques Stettiner* (1927) and certain pictures of 1929, and is vividly illustrated by the drawing here reproduced (above right). It consisted in supplying for several figures, contiguous in head and torso, a common set or sets of legs and arms, fewer in number than the figures would normally have, but so arranged that each figure seems complete. Because of Tchelitchew's masterful draftsmanship, he was able to

16

achieve startling results with "laconic" composition. The system itself is further proof of the painter's originality of vision, being without precedent in modern art and only indirectly prefigured by Dürer's studies of human proportions and by Uccello's battlepieces with their strange confusion of legs and horses' hoofs.

1926–28: The South of France. Algiers. "Ode." First One-Man Exhibition.

In August, 1926, after completing the *Portrait of Natalie Glasko* (plate 7), perhaps the most distinguished of all his portraits done in the subdued color range he had adopted in 1925, Tchelitchew went to the South of France. In his words, "The predominant color of blue in this region surprised me greatly, and gradually indigo, Prussian blue, cerulean and cobalt came to my palette in very dark shadows . . . [seen] against this blue, orange and yellow values appeared as ochre, sienna natural, golden ochre and burnt sienna." In this heightened but still tenebrous key he painted several still lifes of grapes and completed one of the outstanding works of his early career, *The Ship*, already referred to in connection with the lingering effect on his style of the Cubist-Constructivist tradition. The picture is the first in which he painted multiple images (images which are made up of, turn into or suggest other images on close observation). The sky in *The Ship* consists of nine eggs which are at the same time a bunch of grapes; the water is the shadow cast by the egg-grape sky. The picture is thus the direct forerunner of the extraordinary labyrinth of multiple images concealed within *Hide-and-Seek*, and it is significant that in *The Ship*, seemingly the most abstract painting of Tchelitchew's maturity, he should have insisted upon reappraising appearances in terms of representational forms taken from nature.

The sand-coffee-gouache technique utilized in *The Ship* was employed in a majority of his paintings of 1927–28, in "laconic" compositions, nudes (plate 9) and portraits. At times, as in the first of his four portraits of Mrs. Sherman Kent (no. 11), he piled up so heavy a texture that, in his words, "The surface of my painting looked like maps of earth in low relief." He varied this procedure with a less insistent treatment of sand texture, as in two portraits of Miss Edith Sitwell and one of Boris Kochno executed in 1927 and in *Portrait of David Prall* (plate 14) finished in 1928. His subjects' features, though still intensely stylized, were less distorted than before. The volumes were contained by sharp incisions of line rather than by the black, expressionist contours he had previously used. His fine draftsmanship was now allowed to count as never before.

A visit to Algiers in 1927 caused him to lighten his blues still more than he had done in the South of France, and in that city he painted the first pictures of his long series on the circus theme. Among them were *Swinging Acrobats* (collection Stephen Tennant, London) and *Blue Acrobat* (plate 11). He also completed two masked figures, *The Blue Mask* and *The Pink Mask*, both in French collections. On his return from Algiers he painted several versions of a *Man with an Apple* in homage to Cézanne, as well as *The Thinker* (plate 10).

The last-named picture dealt with the figure in relation to its own heavy shadow and to an overlaid linear pattern repeating the figure's outlines. This technique was used in altered form in the sketches he made for the ballet, *Ode*, the following year.

By the latter part of 1927 Tchelitchew had begun to use his sand-coffee-gouache medium with increasing subtlety of tone and texture, painting several still lifes such as *Fruit* (plate 12). Early in 1928 he painted a second portrait of Mrs. Sherman Kent (no. 13), *Soldier with Girl*, *Boy in Striped Sweater* and two or three nudes. These were followed by some still lifes of cabbages of which the one here reproduced (plate 13) is perhaps the finest, being full of warmth and light despite its dark tonality. The cabbage still lifes culminated in a large figure piece, *Boy with Cabbage*. In March, Tchelitchew went to Monte Carlo to design the sets and costumes for *Ode*, now finally commissioned by Diaghilev and destined to win the painter new recognition, as was so often true of artists who worked with the great impresario. Partially as a result of Tchelitchew's success with *Ode* he was given his first one-man exhibition, at the Claridge Gallery, London, in July, 1928. In a comment on the exhibition Miss Edith Sitwell declared: "London has been introduced to a really great new painter, Paul Tchelitchew. And when I say he is a really great painter, I mean what I say. He is not one of these new sensation-mongers that crop up every year, but a painter of the greatest powers, utterly individual, and his work has both majesty and beauty." (Bibl. 31.)

1928–29: Distortions of Perspective. Metamorphic Compositions.

Toward the end of 1928 Tchelitchew completed two paintings, the *Harvester* (plate 15) and *Green Venus* (plate 16), which prefigure the use of distorted recessive perspective to which he has so often turned since 1934. In the *Harvester* the woman's hands, being nearest the observer, are enormously enlarged while her torso diminishes rapidly in scale as it tilts backward into the picture space, culminating in a small head. Similarly the figure in *Green Venus* is shown in foreshortened, exaggerated perspective so that its distortions of form recall images taken from a viewpoint close to the subject by cameras equipped with wide-angle lenses. A third figure piece of the period, a monumental nude entitled *Adam*, reveals an equally arbitrary readjustment of anatomical relationships, notably in the hand of the figure, huge by comparison with its arms, trunk and head. Six years later, in the tennis player and bullfight series of 1934, Tchelitchew was to revive this system of distorted perspective which from then on became a persistent ingredient of his style.

From late 1928, too, dates his sustained interest in metamorphic forms, an interest already implicit in his "laconic" compositions of 1926–27 and in the multiple images of *The Ship*. As a child he had been fascinated by double image postcards, then common in Russia as elsewhere in Europe. Stirred by the memory of these cards and stimulated by the Surrealists' interest in the concealed and ambiguous, he now painted a third gouache and sand portrait of Mrs. Sherman Kent (collection Miss Edith Sitwell) in which his subject's image was several times repeated within the contours of her figure. This was followed in 1929 by a long narrow canvas, the Clown (collection Mrs. R. Gorer, London), in which the clown's body was composed of three child acrobats performing a gymnastic feat. A gouache study for this picture (no. 93) makes clear the transition from "laconic" to metamorphic compositions, for here the arms of the clown are the legs of a flying acrobat while one of the clown's legs becomes both legs of a standing child acrobat. The study's rich, smoldering color and facial characterization suggest that Tchelitchew had looked appreciatively at the gouaches of Georges Rouault, an artist for whom he continues to have the greatest esteem. Possibly it was Rouault's example, too, which led Tchelitchew to the contrapuntal arrangement of dark blues and reds in the Clown Resting (plate 20), a supposition reinforced by the liberal use of black linear overlay in this picture. Yet here as nearly always Tchelitchew has transformed his sources into a conception basically his own.

The metamorphic paintings of 1928–29 reached their climax in the Blue Clown (plate 18) and the Clown (plate 19) both handled in a bright, strongly highlighted blue in contrast to the slumbrous color of the gouache study mentioned above. A drawing for the Blue Clown (plate 17) makes evident how dominant a part metamorphic forms had now come to play in his work. It is an interesting fact that he should have begun to stress these forms in 1929, several years after Max Ernst's first experiments with them but in the very year Salvador Dali began to paint The Invisible Man, full of the trompe l'œil and metamorphosis with which his name has become—exaggeratedly—identified. Although Tchelitchew can certainly claim priority over Dali in depicting multiple images, because of The Ship (1926) and his "laconic" compositions, there is little question that he and Dali arrived at their respective enthusiasms for metamorphosis in complete independence—Dali in Barcelona and Tchelitchew in Paris. Moreover, their conceptions of the significance of metamorphosis were and are wholly different. For while Dali deliberately painted his images so that through a change in the observer's concentration these images would abruptly lose their original identities, becoming a second set of images temporarily blotting out the first, Tchelitchew's aim was opposite. He intended his second and subsequent images to merge with and into the basic form of the picture, never obtruding themselves or obliterating, however momentarily, the outlines and impact of the original theme. Dali, being avowedly anti-esthetic, was primarily interested in the psychic phenomenon of transfixed vision. Tchelitchew on the other hand has always considered that metamorphosis must contribute to fixed structure, that it must be used as a kind of interior magic, creating its own mystery and awe but never becoming a dominant illusion. He wishes the observer to be able to go back and forth easily between hidden images and the composition which contains them, never losing one in seeing the other.

This conscientiousness toward the ancient absolutes of painting did not prevent Tchelitchew's being attacked as a "puzzle-maker" by Jean Cocteau on the occasion of the painter's second one-man show, held at the Galerie Pierre, Paris, in June, 1929. In consequence of this and other adverse criticisms, the artist lost his contract with his dealer and there ensued a period of struggle during which he was sustained by the more consistent faith of his friends and patrons in America and, above all, in England.

The Wire Portraits. Circus Pictures.

Just prior to his Paris exhibition Tchelitchew had finished four sculptured portrait heads consisting of colored wax faces applied to wire forms with open backs. The heads are at once a reminder of his early career as a Constructivist and an indication of how completely he had abandoned the purely abstract approach of the Cubist-Constructivist movement. The portraits included a blue one of Miss Natalie Glasko; one in pink ochre of Miss Edith Sitwell; one in white of Mrs. W. Widney; and a head of a clown in spotted colors. These sculptures were followed by two "laconic" paintings, *Acrobats* and *Two Boys* (collection Geoffrey Gorer, London), the latter being one of the most successful of his pictures of the kind. During the summer of 1929 he continued to work in variations of blue, painting an indigo horse seen against two shadows of its own rearing form, and several gouaches of fallen horses and riders. Late in the year he worked within a narrow range of deep maroons; *Circus Horse* and *The Fall* in the collection of Peter Watson, London, are painted in this tone.

In certain of Tchelitchew's circus paintings of 1929–30 the influence of Picasso's Rose period reached a close point of application. This influence was not merely one of subject matter, though such a subject as that of Tchelitchew's *Burial of the Acrobat* (plate 23) was several times treated by the Spanish master in 1905–06. Rather it consisted primarily in the stylization of the figures and the technique of floating them against a monochromatic variant of their own color, sometimes defining their contours with heavy outlines but often letting the volumes wash loosely against the closely related color of the background. Yet it must immediately be said that Tchelitchew's circus pictures are in no final sense imitative of Picasso's. While the Spaniard's Rose period is marked by a formalism which frequently seems Mannerist, Tchelitchew's vision is more distraught and romantic. During the years when they dealt with the circus theme neither painter was concerned with direct documentation. Both were studio artists, working up their compositions from drawings in which the actual atmosphere and incidents of the circus played only a minor part. But compared to the pathos so brilliantly combined with elegiac serenity in Picasso's Rose paintings, Tchelitchew's mood is darkly metaphysical, even histrionic in the best sense of that word. The difference is not so apparent in the *Burial of the Acrobat* with its ingenious "corkscrew" composition as in the *Fallen Rider* (plate 22) or *The One Who Fell* (plate 24). In both the last-named paintings there is a quality of drama quite different from that which Picasso developed. The former picture's intense convolutions of form are a far cry from Picasso's Rose period calm; the foreshortened figure in the latter painting recalls so "romantic" a Renaissance masterpiece as Mantegna's *Dead Christ* in the Brera rather than the 16th century Mannerist works which anticipate certain of Picasso's Rose period pictures.

Rue de Vaugirard: Still Lifes and Still-Life Figures.

Late in 1929 Tchelitchew had moved into a new apartment on the rue de Vaugirard which he decorated with a dark brown marble mantel and pale blue and yellow walls. To this apartment he one day brought a magnificent bunch of dark red grapes of which he painted a still life (collection Miss Anne Green, Paris) and a metamorphic composition in which the grapes became a reclining clown in a dark red velvet costume (collection Jean Stern, Lausanne). The color of the grapes and the decorations of his apartment were soon reflected in his paintings. He completed six or seven still lifes of apples lying on the brown mantelpiece or in a wire basket and seen against the pale blue background of his studio walls. The largest and most ambitious of these still lifes was entitled *Adoration of the Kings* and had as background an old moving picture theatre then being demolished in the adjoining rue de la Convention. He then painted the still life here reproduced (plate 25) in which first appears the plaster hand soon to become a persistent element in his iconography.

Tchelitchew made a brief trip to England to see the Italian exhibition at the Royal Academy, London, and returned home to work on a series of figure pieces composed of still life. Several months previously he had completed the *Clown Resting* (plate 20) full of an interior imagery of kitchen utensils, as may be seen even more clearly in the drawing of this subject here reproduced (plate 21). The first picture in the new series appears to have been *The Markevitch Family* (collection Edward James, London) in which the heads of the composer and his mother are rendered as portrait canvases within the picture. The composer's portrait head rests on an easel, his torso being made up of drapery and a mesh shopping bag filled with fruit and vegetables. His mother's portrait head rests on the back of a chair curiously like one of the pieces of furniture which Giorgio de Chirico included among the inexplicable bric-à-brac in his canvases of the mid-1920's. The chair and its drapery form Mme. Markevitch's torso. Going back to his system of "laconic" composition, Tchelitchew supplied the two figures with two rather than four hands; both hands are of plaster.

The still-life figure theme was continued in four single figure compositions, two of which must surely rank among the most poetic and convincing pictures of Tchelitchew's career. The first of these was *Still-life Clown* (plate 26) in which the painted portrait head, the torso of bulging shopping bags, and the plaster hand are again utilized, here with exceptional sureness and ingenuity. Next came the *Lawyer* (plate 27), with a draped screen replacing the shopping bag as a torso for the figure. The head image is small in size while the plaster foot in the near foreground is greatly enlarged—a second step toward that distorted perspective which Tchelitchew first used in 1928 and has since vigorously developed. The same arbitrary foreshortening and enlargement are found in the third picture of the still-life figure series, a Neo-Classic scene in which a figure with an enormous plaster hand faces a column with classic bust. The fourth and final painting in the series is *The Annunciation* (collection Miss Edith Sitwell).

During the summer of 1930 Tchelitchew began a new series of still-life figures, distinct from the earlier series in that the portrait heads have disappeared and the mesh shopping bags have become hammocks. There were three paintings in the new series: *Moses* (collection Edward James); *Penelope* (collection the artist, Paris); and *Spanish Dancer* (plate 28). Through that magic with hands which is one of Tchelitchew's distinguishing marks, he has managed to animate these headless figures (the head of *Penelope* is symbolized by a mask) and with sparing use of accessories to suggest clearly the themes which underlie their conception and their titles. All three are painted in the relatively pale colors he had used in the previous series: gray, blue, brown, pink and subtle variants of these tones. This was perhaps the lightest color scale he had used since abandoning his "shocking" palette of 1924–25. It was retained in a grayish pink *Portrait of Edith Sitwell* which followed the still-life figure series, and darkened in the pictures he began early in 1931.

The Spahi Series. "Madame Bonjean." Theatre Subjects.

In the autumn of 1930 Tchelitchew was visited by a friend, George Girard, who had been serving in a Spahi regiment. Impressed by his friend's exotic uniform, the painter made several drawings of him and the following winter (1931) finished the *Seated Spahi* (plate 31) and the *Sleeping Spahi* (plate 32). It seems probable that the *Seated Spahi* came first, since it is far more nearly a portrait than the other and was therefore presumably begun during Girard's visit late in 1930. Furthermore its tonality is lighter and more varied than that of the *Sleeping Spahi*, suggesting that it came soon after the still-life figure series rather than later on when Tchelitchew had darkened and constricted the range of his palette. *Seated Spahi* reveals a new confidence in the artist, a faith in his capacity to alternate the fantastic vocabulary of the still-life figures with an objective simplicity of statement now unmistakably his own. *Sleeping Spahi*, on the other hand, has something of the enigmatic duality of the metamorphic figure pieces of 1929. It is, in the artist's words, his "first human landscape," the forerunner of *Derby Hill Theme: Hiawatha* (no. 67), *Derby Hill Theme: David and Goliath* (color plate, page 77) and other compositions of recent years.

The Spahi series was concluded by a night scene with four figures (collection Lady Juliet Duff, London). While the pervading dark blue of the series was carried over in a few subsequent paintings, for the most part Tchelitchew reverted to the deep wine red he had used the previous year. Ever since 1929 he had been making drawings of a woman spectator at the circus, seated amid clowns, acrobats and the appurtenances of their profession. These sketches now reached final expression in the major composition, *Madame Bonjean* (plate 29). In 1930 he had already achieved a taut and expressive characterization of Mme. Bonjean (no. 26) and he now undertook the difficult task of relating a three-quarter-length figure of the same subject to supplementary circus figures projected into space. Here he was aided by that control of line which not even his most persistent detractors have been able to deny, and by a mastery of atmospheric effect which may some day be recognized as one of his most personal contributions to contemporary art. The figures of Mme. Bonjean and the two acrobats are inexorably fixed, round and deep, and held apart in space by a strengthening of contour in the latter figures as opposed to that of Mme. Bonjean. The short, arbitrary color scale is made to reinforce the linear illusion of a separate spatial existence for each figure, while at the same time acting as a cohesive agent for the over-all composition. Between the acrobats and the net below them there is the dizzy height of the circus top, different in degree for each of the two figures. Mme. Bonjean, on the other hand, is seen straight-on at ground level, an integral part of the spectacle but, as its audience, held away from the performers in position, time and motion. Tchelitchew has recently made the triple presentation of space and time the theoretical basis for his painting, but signs of this preoccupation are latent in the tri-figured composition of *Madame Bonjean*.

After completing a large wine red painting, *The Dream* (collection Stephen Tennant), showing a group of figures peering from beneath the horizon at an outstretched nude male figure, Tchelitchew began work on a series of theatre scenes called "The Loges." The series included *Théâtre français* (plate 33), *Ballet* (private collection, England), and *Concert* (collection Mrs. R. Gorer). In the first-named picture the artist opposed several of his typical, stylized heads to a head realistically drawn almost to the point of caricature—the head of the old man with the opera glasses (said to be the artist, Henri Matisse). Perhaps his rising respect for England and English thought led him to the new pictorialism of this passage and of the picture as a whole. Although his admiration for individual English artists of the past is extremely limited, there is at times an English cast to his romanticism, a connection in spirit with the tradition which runs so waveringly from Hogarth to Aubrey Beardsley. The relationship is primarily one of mind rather than technique, since his painting shows no direct use of English sources.

Tattooed Figures. Final Years of the Circus Theme. "L'Errante."

Tchelitchew's works of 1930 and 1931 were exhibited in a one-man show at the Galerie Vignon, Paris, in June of the latter year. During the summer, after completing several still lifes of flowers, he began the short series of tattooed circus figures which carried through into 1932. His interest in the subject sprang naturally from his concern with interior, multiple images such as those used in the *Blue Clown* and the *Clown* of 1929. Late in 1929 he had begun a still unfinished gouache showing a juggler's back full of metamorphic forms suggested by the subject's muscular structure. Early in 1931 he had executed a second version of the subject, identical in pose and outline, but covered with an imagery which seems by comparison more nearly an applied surface decoration, like tattooing. Now, later in 1931, his interest was attracted anew by the tattooing on the chest and arms of a friend who became the model for the entire series. He treated the subject with that relative objectivity and realism which differentiate the *Seated Spahi* from the *Blue Clown* painted two years earlier, following the model's markings closely, as photographs of the same subject by George Platt Lynes make clear. The tattooing is handled as straight embellishment rather than as metamorphic imagery, and the only ambiguity inherent in his treatment springs from the fact that he was consciously painting pictures of pictures—the tattooed patterns on his friend's skin. The two principal works in the series apart from the one here reproduced (plate 34) are a three-quarter-length oil of the model in black tights and a full-length nude finished in 1932.

The circus continued to supply Tchelitchew's subject matter in a majority of the pictures painted during the latter part of 1932. To this period belong some of the outstanding works of his career, among them the *Musical Clown* (collection Mrs. Edward Maast, London), *Three from the Circus* (collection Prince Dmitri Sturdza, Bucharest), *Head of a Clown* (collection Edward Marsh, London), *Circus Dressing Room* (collection Mrs. R. Gorer), and the *Chinese Song* for which a fine preparatory study is here reproduced (plate 70). It is unfortunate that due to the war none of these paintings is available for the present exhibition, for each illustrates in varying degree the complexity of color with which Tchelitchew now relieved the restricted palette of his earlier career. The clowns of 1932 are usually rendered in high contrasts—green against yellow, blue against rose, with a liberal use of white. They wear bright ruffles and spangled costumes, the latter painted in splashed dots of color which two years later led to the use of sequins affixed to the canvas (plate 38). The naturalism of these works by comparison with earlier paintings is even more evident in still lifes of the period.

Tchelitchew's technique was becoming less and less mannered, and the deliberate mystification of his years as one of the Neo-Romantic *tenebrosi* was now increasingly a thing of the past. He still carried with him a romantic predilection for atmosphere and mood but this was now extrinsic—comparatively speaking—and qualified to a limited degree by what he saw around him. His reaction to the more bizarre aspects of the contemporary world though still put through a process of formalization, was growing more direct and spontaneous. Indeed certain of his 1932 canvases are related to those of an artist who reacted to his age more violently than did most of his contemporaries—Henri de Toulouse-Lautrec. Tchelitchew's art is far less "actual" than Lautrec's, of course, but the regard he has so long professed for the French master is reflected in his clown pictures of this period. It may be felt in his summary, harsh characterization of faces, in the gaslight colors—greens, blues and yellows—which these faces absorb as a strange pallor, and in the bursts of raw pigment with which the costumes of his clowns are sometimes treated. Two years later Lautrec was again to contribute to Tchelitchew's inspiration, but in the latter's paintings of 1932 may be seen signs of that affinity between the two artists upon which Tchelitchew has often insisted.

Sometime during the year 1932 the painter executed a number of drawings in which cloud-forms turn into all manner of fantastic images. These drawings prefigure the metamorphic landscapes of 1940–41 (plates 72 and 73), but were never developed into paintings at this time. Instead Tchelitchew finished a large gouache, *Girl with Lilacs* (collection Edward James) and did several large preliminary studies for a big composition of male figures entitled *The Bathers* (collection Mrs. R. Gorer) which was completed in 1933. *The Bathers* was followed by *Three Sitting Together* (plate 35) and by the picture which was the climax of

24

Tchelitchew's preoccupation with the circus. This was *The Concert* (plate 36), remarkable for its compositional balance, luminosity and tenderness of conception. It was Tchelitchew's farewell to the circus and a worthy one. He never again made the subject a central theme in his painting.

During the winter of 1933 the artist worked on the décor and costumes for the ballet, *L'Errante*, produced as part of the "Ballets 1933" program in Paris the following spring. The décor was achieved almost exclusively through an original and sensitive use of lights against curtained backdrops. Unlike those School of Paris painters who were content to have their easel sketches enlarged, erected on the stage and generously spotlighted, Tchelitchew approached stage design organically in *L'Errante*, concerning himself with all the mechanics of stagecraft and using them with great mastery. (His early experience as a Constructivist stood him in good stead.) For the very reason that his conception of the stage's problems is so well integrated, complete and self-contained, his work in the theatre has never affected his work as an easel painter. At times he has simultaneously designed ambitious stage productions and executed large-scale compositions in oil or gouache, and neither effort has shown a trace of the other. He does not transfer pictures to the stage and, more important still, he never permits the theatre to infect his paintings with its specialized drama and artifice. He understands instinctively and as a matter of theory that there are things which may be said in the one place and not in the other. The distinction is less easily made than might be supposed.

1933: Portraits. 1934: The Tennis Players and the Bullfight Series.

To the latter part of 1933 belong three portraits of the African dancer, Féral Benga, among them *The Mask of Light* (no. 39). At this time Tchelitchew also executed several portraits of Charles Henri Ford, one of which served as a study for *The Ascension* (collection Edward James) finished early in 1934. A second portrait of the poet (plate 37) is painted against the light, giving an halation to the contours of the figure and making some of the volumes transparent. Within the shadowed face the eyes are an extremely luminous blue, illustrating what was to become one of the artist's chief ambitions—to give pigment its own inner phosphorescence, so that a given picture will appear to light itself from beneath its surface. Through long and conscientious development, the blue light of the poet's eyes has led to the mysterious incandescence of whole sections of *Hide-and-Seek*.

After completing a small oil, *Dream of the Girl*, whose eerie, *Turn of the Screw* romanticism pervades many of the painter's studies of children, Tchelitchew began work on a major theme—"the tennis players." He commenced with two very large pastel heads of a baby tennis player, *Peter the Great* (plate 39) and *Head of a Child* (collection Edward James), drawn with a control of linear modeling which recalls Paolo Uccello. These pastels were accompanied by numerous drawings, many of which were side views of the head of a girl with an enormously enlarged ear. Gradually the figure of the girl, three-quarter-length and seen in violently distorted perspective, became the subject of the final version of *The Tennis Players* (plate 40). (It is the same girl, remembered from childhood, who appears at intervals in the artist's work and rests against the middle of the tree trunk in *Hide-and-Seek*.) In another version of the subject (no. 36) the baby tennis player becomes the main protagonist with the girl as his opponent in the background. In this form the tennis player theme took its place in the complicated iconography of *Phenomena*. In both versions the exaggerated perspective first developed in the *Green Venus* and the *Harvester* of 1928 has now supplied a dominant approach to the problem of spatial relationships.

In the summer of 1934 Tchelitchew went to Spain, which in his words, "produced an enormous impression. . . . The dry mother-of-pearl landscape of northern Spain, the characteristic proud faces of men and women, dressed in dark clothes, the bullfights, the towns, the Arabian vestiges, all combined to induce me to take a wholly new direction." Like Delacroix before him, he was transfixed by the intensity of light and by the dramatic quality of the landscape, the architecture and the people. After a short period of travel he settled in a small fishing village, Fuengerola, in the province of Malaga. There he first conceived the idea of presenting subject matter as seen simultaneously from three different angles of perspective— from below, straight-on and from above. The principle of simultaneity was not to be applied to a single object, as it had been in his multiple figures of 1926–27. Instead each object was to be rendered as a single image seen from a fixed viewpoint. But the viewpoint was to change from one object to the next, and within the same composition any object was to be represented as seen from any one of the three perspectives which suited his purpose. He promptly applied this system of triple perspective to three gouaches of bullfights. Only one of these—the least illustrative of the principle involved—is available for the present exhibition (plate 41).

In the writer's opinion none of the three pictures deserves to rank with Tchelitchew's finest work, partly as a result of architectonic difficulties not then fully resolved, partly because in certain passages the color seems to overrun its function. But no one could expect immediate success with so revolutionary a use of perspective, and there are passages in all three paintings which deserve scrutiny rather than cursory dismissal. One of these passages is the huge ear of the foreground figure in the gouache here reproduced. Viewed purely as a tour de force, its transparency and luminosity are uncanny, particularly for an opaque medium like gouache. The passage is related to the head of the girl in *The Tennis Players* and beyond that to the glowing, gas-lit faces, penetrated by a light coming from beneath, which Toulouse-Lautrec used in certain of his music hall compositions such as *At the Moulin Rouge* (The Art Institute of Chicago). By Tchelitchew's own word it was Lautrec's example which led him to his interest in the effect of light coming through flesh. His use of a large-scale head at the extreme edge of the foreground may also have been inspired by the French master.

It is the foreground figure with the large ear which sets the key for the triple perspective in *The Bullfight*. This figure is seen from above. Behind it to the right of the picture the angle of vision drops to normal, so that the bull and bullfighter in that section are viewed straight-on. At the left of the composition, the angle of vision drops to the ground and the foreground bullfighter is seen in elongated, distorted perspective. Here, then, is the beginning of Tchelitchew's triple perspective, repeatedly used since 1934, reaching its culmination in *Phenomena*, but retained in modified form in even more recent paintings.

Arrival in America. One-Man Exhibition. Revival of "L'Errante." Italy.

On leaving Spain Tchelitchew stopped briefly in Paris, where he painted a portrait of Mme. Helena Rubinstein (plate 38) with green and white sequins affixed to the canvas giving its surface a mosaic effect. He came to America in October, 1934, and in December had his first one-man exhibition in this country, at the Julien Levy Gallery, New York. The following spring he collaborated on a new production of his 1933 ballet, *L'Errante*, for which all the sketches included in the present exhibition were prepared (nos. 198-203).

In May, 1935, Tchelitchew went to London and thence to Italy, a country he had never before visited. The latter fact is significant in view of his identification with Neo-Romanticism and particularly with Christian Bérard and Eugène Berman who had found their original impetus in that movement. For while Bérard and Berman had travelled widely and frequently in Italy since 1926, finding in Piero della Francesca, Raphael and the muralists of Ferrara an Italianate basis for their own painting, Tchelitchew had worked in Paris and London. The point has been made elsewhere (bibl. 39) but may be repeated here, that Tchelitchew's romanticism by comparison with theirs is Northern both stylistically and in metaphysical approach. Though there are certain Italian artists to whom his affinity is apparent—notably Tintoretto and, above all, Uccello whose influence on Tchelitchew's arbitrary distortions of perspective is not to be minimized—his relation to the early Germanic and Flemish masters, even to a later English fantasist like Richard Dadd, often seems closer. In thinking of Tchelitchew's art in terms of fairly direct analogy, the name of Grünewald comes to mind rather than that of Raphael; that of Altdorfer or Bruegel rather than that of Piero della Francesca or Titian. Tiepolo, profoundly admired by Bérard and Berman, has never been one of Tchelitchew's favorite artists. Instead Tchelitchew's inspiration carries strong traces of the diabolism which welled up in England and Germany in Tiepolo's time. And it is significant that he has so long and consciously rebelled against the canons of sensibility and taste evolved by the French tradition in opposition to the elaboration and extravagance of "les barbares" across the Channel and the Rhine. From the very beginning of his career he has rejected the conception of painting as an art of sensuous pleasure which seems so typically French. He did so in his "laconic" compositions of 1926–27; he has done so lately in *Hide-and-Seek*. But his most forceful, if not his most successful, protest against "taste" was made in the huge canvas, *Phenomena* (plate 53).

1935–38: The Beginning of "Phenomena." The Paper Ball. The Ballets "Magic" and "Orpheus." Portraits.

According to the artist, the inspiration for *Phenomena* came to him first as he looked at the famous bronze door of the church of San Zeno Maggiore at Verona. Leaving that city after a tour which took him throughout Italy, he settled at Malcesine on Lake Garda and there executed the drawing, *Beggars' Lane* (no. 126), with the door of San Zeno Maggiore in mind. He next completed nearly thirty-five gouaches of figures and scenes, most of which later found their way into *Phenomena*. Among them were *The Bathers—I* (plate 42), *The Bathers—II* (no. 42), and *The Lorelei* (no. 44). He also did a series of small oils later utilized in the composition of *Phenomena*. *Leopard Boy* (plate 46) and *Pip and Flip* (plate 45) are typical of the series, and one has only to look at them to realize how far Tchelitchew had left behind the open pathos of his early career as a Neo-Romantic. Their ruthless commentary on the freakish aspects of contemporary civilization removes them immeasurably from the clowns of 1929–30, reclining in melancholy torpor. Tchelitchew's oils and gouaches of 1935 are the work of a man roused from despair and somnambulist escape to speak in harsh accents against the defacement, cheapness and contradictions of his era. They are images springing from nerves rubbed raw, expressed through a fantasy which is in part instinctive and generic, in part consciously satirical.

From 1935 to 1938 Tchelitchew worked steadily on sketches for *Phenomena* (nos. 127, 131, 132, 152) and after August, 1936, on the canvas itself. At the same time he accomplished additional work which alone would have exhausted a less ambitious painter. In February, 1936, he executed the décor for the Paper Ball held in the Avery Memorial Museum of the Wadsworth Atheneum, Hartford. He transformed the entire court of the building into a circus setting by covering its walls with newspapers on which he applied decorations and figures. He also designed paper costumes for many of the participants in the Ball and did the set and costumes for a one-act ballet, *Magic*, held in the Avery Auditorium. In the spring of the same year he designed the décor and costumes for the ballet, *Orpheus*, produced in New York. He then returned to Italy, where at Santa Margherita Ligure he evolved his final conception of *Phenomena*.

During his stay in Italy and later in Paris Tchelitchew painted several portraits with wide stripes as a decorative motif of which the *Portrait of Edith Sitwell* (plate 47) is incomparably the most important. Returning to America, he continued to work on *Phenomena* and to paint portraits in which a new clarity and delicacy of contour may be partly attributed to his deep interest in silverpoint, a medium he had begun to use extensively toward the end of 1936 (nos. 133, 138, 141). A majority of these portraits were painted in the dry, bright colors he had adopted in the oil sketches for *Phenomena*; often several images of his subject were depicted, as in the *Portrait of Lincoln Kirstein* (plate 48). Slightly later, he began the extremely fine *Portrait of Constance Askew* (plate 49) and in it reverted to a darker palette and richer surface while retaining the precision of linear modeling to which his use of silverpoint had led him.

28

"Phenomena."

By the spring of 1938 *Phenomena* was finished and exhibited at Arthur Tooth & Sons, London, where it created an uproar which increased in intensity when the picture was shown in New York the following autumn. With few exceptions critics attacked the canvas bitterly, summoning a vocabulary of invective to which moral fervor contributed some of the most colorful and irrelevant phrases. The extraordinary invention of incident within the picture, which may constitute its chief importance whether "literary" in inspiration or not, was dismissed as decadent and extra-pictorial. But it may be that today, when an interest in iconology is being revived at the hands of Renaissance scholars and spreading to the contemporary field, *Phenomena* will be given the more detailed study it has always deserved.

It is a picture which can only be read piecemeal, and this is a fault which no amount of iconographic interest can entirely obviate and which makes *Phenomena* seem a far lesser accomplishment than *Hide-and-Seek*. Yet the artist had made exceptionally elaborate plans to give the canvas cohesion and unity. To begin with, the composition is based on a pyramidal form repeated in all directions like the facets of a diamond. In addition, the color is intended to act as a unifying force, being applied as a rainbow spectrum in reverse, from bottom to top and from right to left, from cold and bright to pale and warm. In the final oil sketch for the painting (plate 52), both the pyramidal structure and the rainbow waves of color do in fact contribute a unity and over-all impact which make this picture more satisfactory compositionally than *Phenomena* itself. For in the large painting an overcrowding and heightened realism of detail tend to disrupt continuity and break the canvas up into isolated fragments, to be read as a running scenario, close-to. Yet these fragments, though marred occasionally by malice in satire's place, are frequently fine in invention and handling; what they lack in epic quality is often compensated for by the nervous vigor of their conception and by their technical brilliance. Surely only the dogmatic can dismiss *Phenomena* completely as so many dismissed it when it was first shown. And for the rising iconographers whose influence on criticism may be felt increasingly, the picture is a rich field for investigation. In it there are famous people and freaks, commentary within commentary, and running through the whole a juxtaposition of opposites—rich to poor, large to small, light to dark, and so on to the very fibre of antithesis. Finally, from the point of view of the artist's own development, *Phenomena* was invaluable in that it freed his abnormally sensitive imagination from a superabundance of irritants and fantasies, leaving him free to work with a new strength and monumentality, as *Hide-and-Seek* so visibly attests.

"St. Francis." "Ondine." Connecticut, 1938–40.

During the spring of 1938 Tchelitchew worked on sketches for the décor and costumes of the ballet, *St. Francis* (no. 209), which contributed a new and poignant romanticism to the

PHelithew
1938

Figures in Landscape, 1938. Ink. Collection the artist. *Not included in exhibition.*

theatre and marked one of the high points of his career as stage designer. He afterwards travelled briefly in the Balkans, but a serious illness forced him to return to America and he settled in the country at Weston, Connecticut. Back in Paris for the summer of 1939, he created the décor and costumes for Louis Jouvet's production of *Ondine* by Jean Giraudoux, which aroused wide and enthusiastic comment. Because of his poor health he lived in the country at St. Jorioz near Lac d'Annecy. The mountains of this region inspired him to paint landscapes which are at the same time human bodies. Here he painted an oil of the hills as lovers, *Fata Morgana*. A fine preparatory watercolor of this subject is included in the present exhibition (no. 160). Here, too, he conceived the theme of *Boys Fighting in Wheat*, painting an oil (plate 56) and a gouache (no. 56). The theme was later utilized in *The Green Lion* (plate 57) and in a section of *Hide-and-Seek*. He also completed several gouache studies later incorporated in the composition of the last-named canvas.

It was the New England countryside of the Westport region which had first turned his attention to landscape and to the metamorphic forms lurking within the swells and hollows of the land. The previous fall (1938) he had been moved profoundly by the variety and richness of color of the New England autumn and had covered the walls of his studio with leaves and with innumerable studies of them executed with the utmost precision of detail (nos. 161 and 169). Gradually he had come to see in these leaves, particularly in oak leaves frozen by winter and clinging stubbornly to their branches, the shapes of children in fantastic cloaks (plate 54). At the same time the snowy landscape had suggested the shapes of various animals

30

—a polar bear and leopard in combat and later, in *Portrait of My Father* (plate 50), a tiger. When he returned to Weston for the fall and winter of 1939–40, these visual phenomena fascinated him anew and provided the subjects for nearly all his paintings and drawings (e.g. plate 55). Thus he returned again to that exploration of metamorphosis which had occupied him eleven years earlier.

It was now nature rather than the figure of man which supplied basic forms suggestive of other appearances. And Tchelitchew's attitude toward nature is surprisingly reverent for a man of his urbanity, though understandable in view of the deep superstition which governs so much of his thought. In turning so directly to nature for metamorphic inspiration, he has taken his place in the long tradition which stretches from certain Italian fantasists of the 16th and 17th centuries to a modern English illustrator like Arthur Rackham. But he has brought to the transcription of metamorphosis a sternness of ambition, an acuteness of sub-conscious recognition, and a compositional sense which have saved him from a dangerous over-dependence on *trompe l'œil* for its own limited sake. It is this fact which gives the best of his recent paintings and drawings a quality of revelation rather than of invention and makes comparison with more literary fantasists like Rackham meaningless, or at best superficial. On the other hand, his treatment of metamorphosis at times closely parallels that of Max Ernst, whose work has the same intuitive magic, the same effective combination of conscious elegance and free discovery.

The impact of New England's autumn foliage has been assuredly the most important factor contributing to the brilliance of color in Tchelitchew's recent landscapes and in the various studies for *Hide-and-Seek*. There is, however, another factor which demands mention: the influence of the young Chilean painter, Matta, who arrived in America from Paris in 1939 and whose extremely original use of color has already affected numerous painters of the first rank. It should at once be said that Tchelitchew has never compromised his own highly personal vision by an overclose dependence upon Matta. Nevertheless, he has certainly done what so many 20th century painters have done before him—the name of Picasso comes instantly to mind—that is, he has refreshed his technique through qualified admiration for the work of a younger artist. Within definite limits of application, the influence of Matta on Tchelitchew is unmistakable. It shows in the new fluidity of color in the *Head of Autumn* (plate 63); it consists in an amorphous "wash" handling of pigment in certain passages of recent works and in a tropical brightness of tone, particularly in the yellows, reds and greens. It reached its highest point in 1940–41, and since then has receded, becoming absorbed as a minor element in the technical mastery which the painter has earned through years of experiment and work on his own part.

The Derby Hill Landscapes. Recent Ballets.

During the summer of 1940, spent in Vermont, Tchelitchew began a series of landscapes, inspired by a view of Derby Hill, called "Theme and Three Variations." The theme picture (no. 72) has only just been completed, but the first variation, *Hiawatha* (no. 67) was finished in 1940. The second variation, *David and Goliath*, also but recently completed though begun in 1941, is here reproduced in color (page 77); the third is *Niobe* (no. 74). Of the first-named three, *David and Goliath*, with its strange rapport between the sharply outlined tree-figure at the left and the giant half concealed in the hills, seems by far the finest. All three pictures, despite their metamorphic overtones, illustrate the directness of interpretation that Tchelitchew employs at intervals as a foil to projects in which fantasy plays a more insistent part. By comparison with any of the multiple image landscape drawings he made in Vermont during the summer of 1941 (plates 72 and 73), these paintings are indeed "straight" transcriptions of a contemporary scene—the painter's devotional offering to the confidante whom he calls "Mrs. Nature."

In 1941 Tchelitchew designed the décor and costumes for the ballets, *Balustrade* and *Cave of Sleep*. In June, 1942, he designed the décor and costumes for two ballets with choreography by George Balanchine, presented at the *Théâtre Colon* in Buenos Aires: the first was *Apollon Musagète*, with music by Stravinsky; the second, *Concerto*, danced to selections from Mozart. Meanwhile he had been working with tremendous concentration on *Hide-and-Seek* (plate 68), surely his masterwork to date.

"Hide-and-Seek."

The canvas itself was begun at Derby Hill in the summer of 1940, but its genesis really dates from the spring of 1934 when, on a friend's estate in Sussex, England, Tchelitchew saw a huge, gnarled tree of which he made a literal sketch (plate 58). The tree, with its finger-like branches, remained in his thought and the following year he peopled it with children playing hide-and-seek, executing a drawing (plate 59) and a gouache (collection Edward James). For the next three years the hide-and-seek theme lay dormant in his mind as he worked on *Phenomena*. His interest was revived at Weston in 1938–39 by the autumn leaves which he saw as capes concealing the forms of children, and there he made a drawing showing the hand-like Sussex tree as a double hand (plate 60). Almost immediately he rejected the idea of the tree as a double hand for the simple yet unanswerable reason that, in his words, "it was too much." He thereupon made a magnificent ink and water color sketch of the tree as it finally appears in *Hide-and-Seek*, that is, a tree with branches forming a hand and with a human foot for its base (plate 61). As he transferred this conception of the tree to the canvas, he gradually perceived that the trunk was suggestive of an old man's head seen full-face, with the branches of the tree as wild hair. In time he therefore arrived at the central multiple image of *Hide-and-Seek*: the tree as a joined hand and foot, and also as the head of an aged Viking, with its left eye formed by the butterfly on the tree trunk, its right eye by the arm of the girl spread-eagled against the trunk, its nose by the girl's torso.

By the summer of 1940 the disposition of the passages surrounding the tree and interlacing its finger-branches had become relatively clear in his mind, as a drawing from this period indicates (plate 67). There were to be two principal children's heads, representing seasons of the year, facing each other across the tree trunk—at the left (from the observer's view-point) "Head of Spring" (frontispiece), at the right "Head of Autumn" (plate 66). In the drawing mentioned above, there are five children's heads or heads-and-figures woven into the finger-branches above the heads of spring and autumn. This number was increased to six in the final canvas. (The head which in the drawing appears beneath the "Head of Autumn" was moved up to a position between the fourth and little fingers of the tree.) Five of these heads are seen from above, at relatively the same angle from which the baby at the foot of the tree is seen. The sixth, "Head of Summer," is seen more nearly straight-on and acts as a transi-tional passage between the five heads in the branches and the heads of spring and autumn which are viewed at normal eye level. It is to be observed that in *Hide-and-Seek* Tchelitchew's system of triple perspective, though stressed in the artist's rationalization of the picture quoted later in this text, has in fact been drastically modified. His use of perspective in depicting various images within *Hide-and-Seek* is still arbitrary and changeable but does not follow the triple sequence of the bullfight paintings of 1934 or, to a lesser degree, of *Phenomena*. The clear structural solidity which makes the composition of *Hide-and-Seek* less intrusive and forced than that of *Phenomena* must be partially ascribed to this modification.

Counting the baby at the foot of the tree, the children's heads or heads-and-figures in *Hide-and-Seek* add up to nine, the same number Tchelitchew had used sixteen years before for the egg-grapes which form the sky in *The Ship*. The evolution of the heads of spring and autumn is fully documented in the present exhibition (nos. 172-174; 178-182), as is that of the two images next in importance, the "Head of Summer" (plate 65) and "The Drop of Water" (plate 64), the latter being a baby's head which forms a landscape and pool of water. Read in chronological order, each of these series of studies reveals a common procedure: in each Tchelitchew worked toward a multiplication of metamorphic imagery which he carried still further in *Hide-and-Seek* itself. Despite this ultimate complication of motif he achieved a higher degree of technical precision in the big canvas than in even so finished a preliminary study as the *Head of Spring* (plate 62). But whereas the greater realism and abundance of detail in *Phenomena*, by comparison with its final sketch, had tended to disrupt the picture's unity and scatter its interest, here the opposite is true. From the studies for *Hide-and-Seek* to the final canvas, Tchelitchew moved steadily toward an ever more impressive clarity, unity and grandeur. The picture is all in one piece and so it may be seen before the observer begins that exploration of its interior images which leads to almost endless discoveries. The fact is the more remarkable in that this—a very large and complicated composition—was begun and finished on the canvas without measurement or calculation as to the scale of the component parts.

Nearly all the passages of *Hide-and-Seek* have specific antecedents in Tchelitchew's work of the past three years and are the result of long and conscientious development. Thus the figure at the top middle of the composition, between the index and second fingers, derives from his studies of boys fighting amid wheat and also from *The Green Lion*, though the lion form itself has disappeared. The figure of the burning boy, between the second and third fingers, appears to have been a complete improvisation, but the fighting leaf-children around the little finger were treated in numerous canvases and drawings of 1939–41. The delicate tracery of the branches above the leaf-children was prefigured but never so well realized in earlier pictures. For sheer wonder of handling it constitutes one of the most rewarding passages in the entire canvas, rivaled only by the miraculous translucence of the lower right section defining the back of the figure of autumn. The new-born baby at the foot of the tree is clearly a development of the fine pastel heads of 1934, *Peter the Great* and *Head of a Child*.

Tchelitchew's theory of the requisite function of painting has been affected, as has that of other of his most distinguished contemporaries, by Einstein's Time-Space theory. This is not to say that he or his fellow-artists have studied the theory except in its broadest implications, but that like painters in centuries past they have been sensitive to a current of thought before it has passed from the scholastic circles of its origin to general acceptance and understanding. (Their respect for Einstein's theory provides an interesting analogy to the respect the Impressionists had for the physical science of optics which was a natural complement to the materialism of the 19th century.) For *Hide-and-Seek* Tchelitchew has therefore evolved a theory of metamorphosis which he defines as follows: "It consists in three different subjects happening in three separate moments of time and seen from three points of view which must correspond to the three levels of perspective: above, straight-on, and below. In this manner each point of view is attached to a separate moment of time, which in the condition of metamorphosis inhering in the painting exist as one, simultaneously, indivisibly and independently."

How authentic the application of the Time-Space theory to contemporary art has been, is a matter which must await further evidence and later analysis. Certainly *Hide-and-Seek* should survive the decision whatever it may be, since the painting needs no such intricate rationalization. Indeed it is difficult to resist making the conjecture that *Hide-and-Seek* may join the small group of large modern pictures to which the word "masterpiece" applies with something of its old, pre-slogan force. The painting's claim to a place in this group is hardly a matter of size, for contemporary art is replete with large-scale works in which painters have magnified what was well enough seen before. But there are a few big modern pictures into which the artist has been able to funnel a new and concentrated inspiration, slowly or quickly, easily or in torment, but always with certainty of hand and eye and with unrelenting pressure from the sources of his volition. Tchelitchew seems to have done precisely this in *Hide-and-Seek*. Given his integrity and devotion, his willingness to court failure for the privilege of ignoring it completely in the end, it may be that he will do paintings of like rank in the future. Within a short time he will begin work on another large composition. It is to be entitled *Paradise*.

34

PLATES

1. Prostitutes, 1925. Oil on canvas. Private collection, Paris. *Not included in exhibition.*

2. Portrait, 1925. Oil on canvas. Private collection, Paris. *Not included in exhibition.*

3. Basket of Strawberries, 1925. Oil on canvas, 15 x 18⅛". Collection Allen Porter, New York.

4. Multiple Heads, 1925. Oil on canvas. Private collection, Paris. *Not included in exhibition.*

5. Eggs, 1925. Oil on canvas. Private collection, Paris. *Not included in exhibition.*

6. Nude in Space, 1926. Oil and sand on canvas. Collection Marcel Kanne, Paris. *Not included in exhibition.*

7. Portrait of Natalie Glasko, 1926. Oil on canvas. Collection Pierre Loeb, Paris. *Not included in exhibition*.

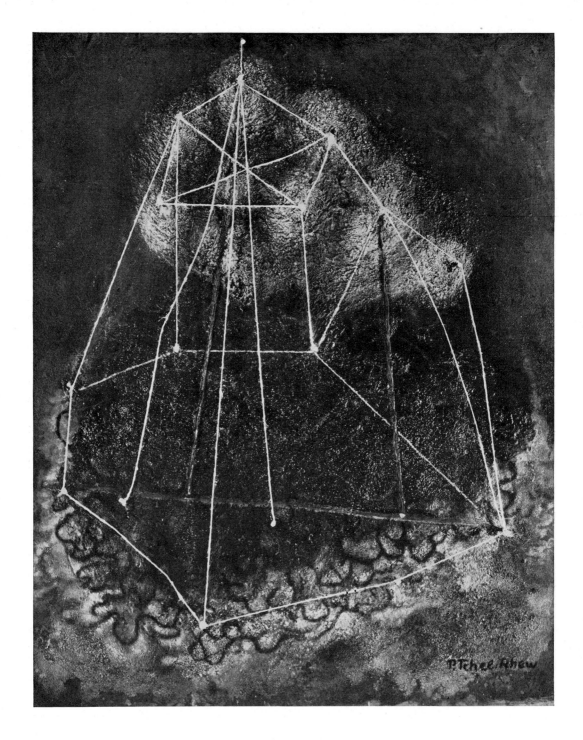

8. The Ship, 1926. Gouache, sand and coffee, 36½ x 28¾". Collection Mr. and Mrs. Sherman Kent, Washington, D.C.

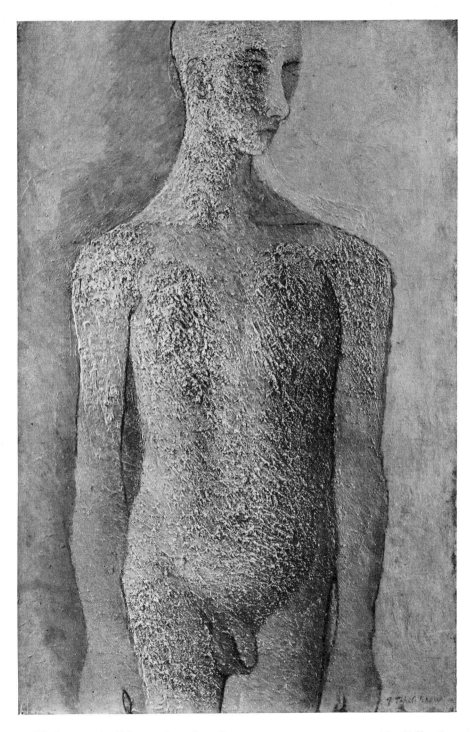

9. Nude, 1926. Oil, sand and coffee on canvas, 39⅛ x 25¼″. Collection Julien Levy, New York.

10. The Thinker, 1927. Gouache, sand and coffee, 24¾ x 19". Collection Mr. and Mrs. Sherman Kent, Washington, D.C.

11. Blue Acrobat, 1927. Gouache, sand and coffee, 24⅞ x 18⅞". Collection Mr. and Mrs. Sherman Kent, Washington, D.C.

12. Fruit, 1927. Gouache and sand, 14¼ x 19¼". Collection Mrs. Charles H. Russell, Jr., New York.

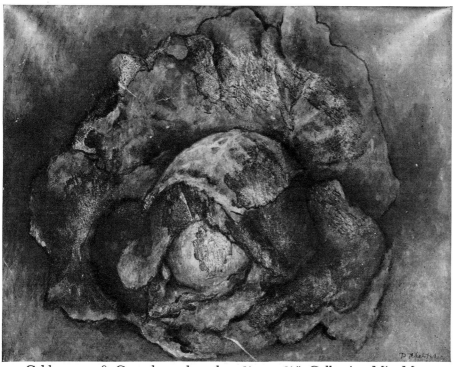

13. Cabbage, 1928. Gouache and sand, 19⅝ x 25⅝". Collection Miss Margaret C. Prall, Berkeley, California.

43

14. Portrait of David Prall, 1928. Oil on canvas, 25½ x 19¾". Collection Miss Margaret C. Prall, Berkeley, California.

15. Harvester, 1928. Oil on canvas. Collection Pierre Loeb, Paris. *Not included in exhibition.*

16. Green Venus, 1928. Oil on canvas. Collection Miss Edith Sitwell, London. *Not included in exhibition.*

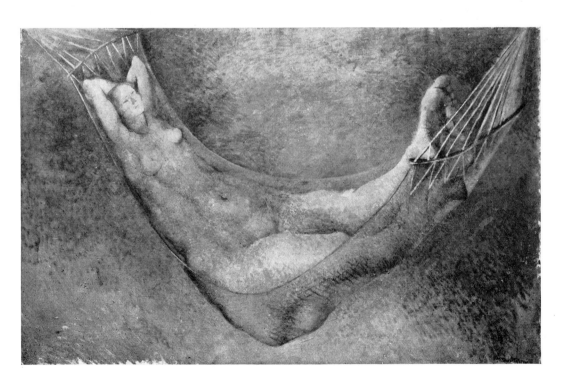

17. Study for the Blue Clown, 1929. Ink wash, 16 x 10½". The Museum of Modern Art, New York, Mrs. Simon Guggenheim Fund.

18. Blue Clown, 1929. Oil on canvas, 31 ¾ x 23 ⅝ ". Private collection.

19. Clown, 1929. Oil on canvas, 29½ x 17½″. Collection Mr. and Mrs. Sherman Kent, Washington, D.C.

20. Clown Resting, 1930. Gouache, 15¾ x 31¼″. Collection Maurice J. Speiser, New York.

21. Study after the Clown Resting, 1930. Brown ink wash, 8½ x 16½″. Julien Levy Gallery, New York.

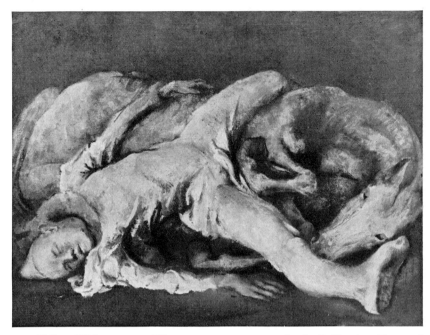

22. Fallen Rider, 1930. Oil on canvas, 21¼ x 28¾". Collection Bernard Davis, Philadelphia.

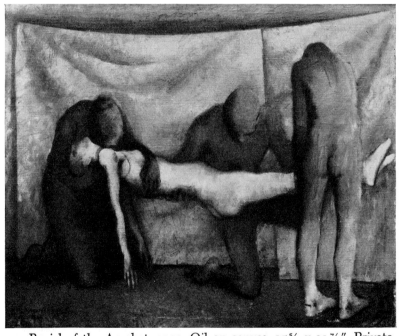

23. Burial of the Acrobat, 1930. Oil on canvas, 25⅝ x 31⅞". Private collection.

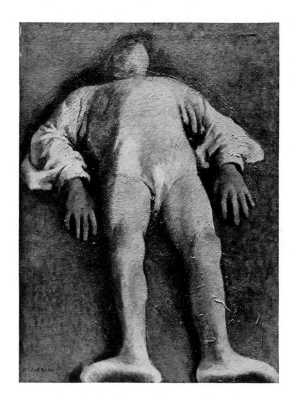

24. The One Who Fell, 1930. Oil on canvas. Collection The Hon. Stephen Tennant, London. *Not included in exhibition.*

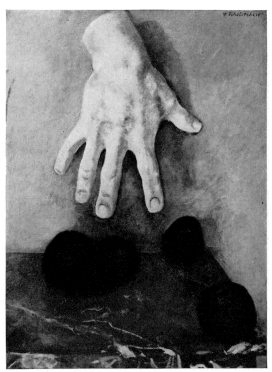

25. Plaster Hand, 1930. Oil on canvas, 32 x 23¾". Julien Levy Gallery, New York.

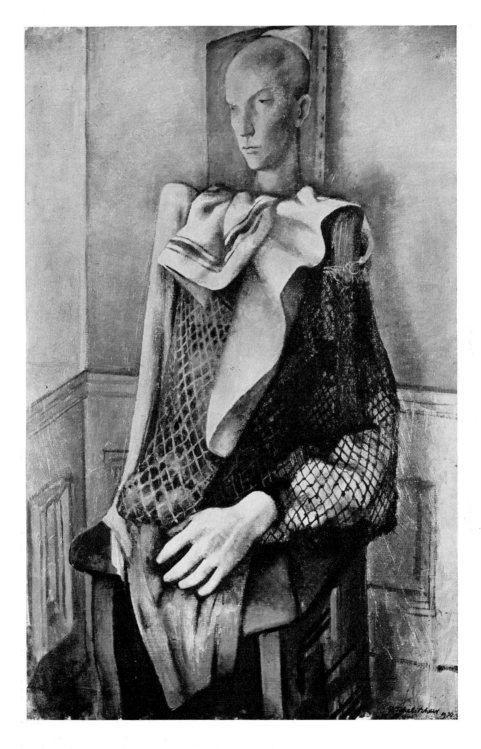

26. Still-life Clown, 1930. Oil on canvas, 39⅜ x 25⅝". Private collection.

27. Lawyer, 1930. Oil on canvas. Collection Sidney Schiff, London. *Not in-cluded in exhibition.*

28. Spanish Dancer, 1930. Oil on canvas, 38 x 28½″. Julien Levy Gallery, New York.

29. Madame Bonjean, 1931. Oil on canvas, 51¼ x 38¼". Private collection.

30. Natalie Paley as Ophelia, 1932. Oil on canvas, 32 x 23¾". Collection Mr. and Mrs. John C. Wilson, New York.

31. Seated Spahi, 1931. Oil on canvas, 36¼ x 28¾". Julien Levy Gallery, New York.

32. Sleeping Spahi, 1931. Gouache, 29⅜ x 40⅝". Private collection.

33. Théâtre français, 1931. Oil on canvas, 29½ x 40″. Collection Mr. and Mrs. John E. Abbott, New York.

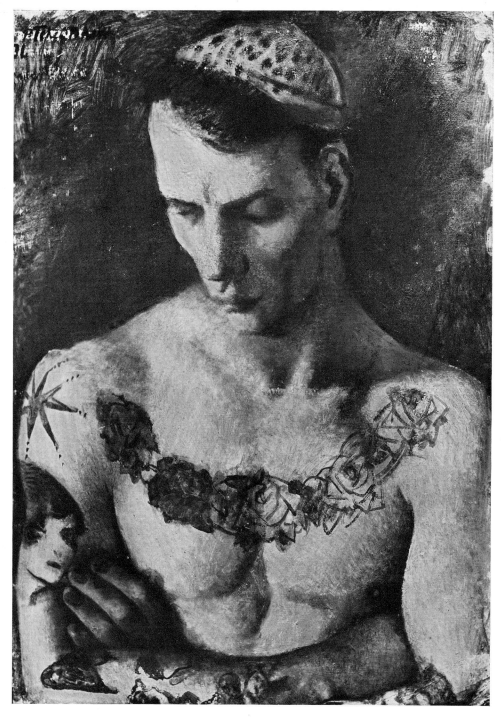

34. The Rose Necklace, 1931. Oil on canvas. Collection Mrs. Edward Maast, London. *Not included in exhibition.*

35. Three Sitting Together, 1933. Oil on beaverboard, 29⅝ x 41½". Collection the artist.

36. The Concert, 1933. Oil on canvas. Collection Edward James, London. *Not included in exhibition.*

37. Portrait of Charles Henri Ford, 1933. Oil on canvas, 39⅝ x 28⅞". Collection Charles Henri Ford, New York.

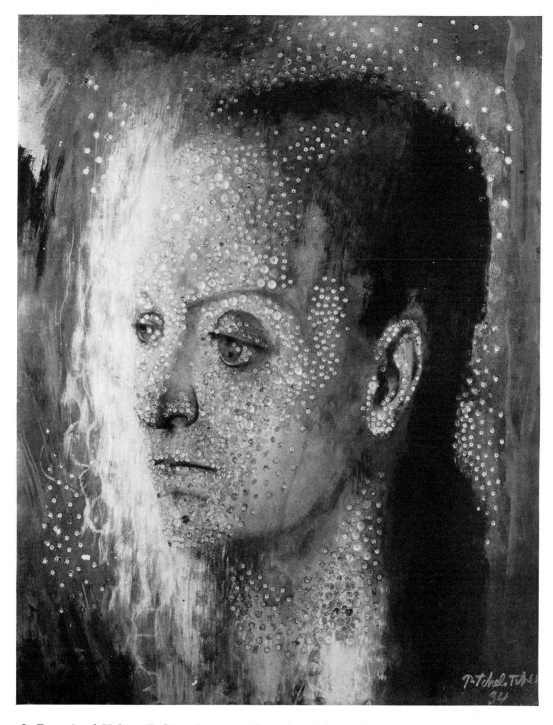

38. Portrait of Helena Rubinstein, 1934. Gouache with sequins, 25 x 20″. Collection Mme. Helena Rubinstein, New York.

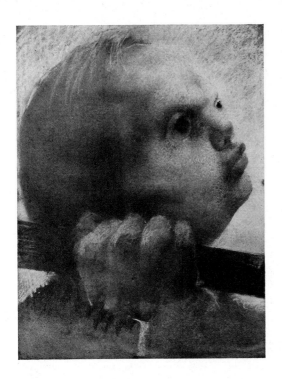

39. Peter the Great, 1934. Pastel. Collection Edward James, London. *Not included in exhibition.*

40. The Tennis Players, 1934. Oil on canvas. Collection Sir Kenneth Clark, London. *Not included in exhibition.*

64

41. Bullfight, 1934. Gouache, 41½ x 29⅝". Julien Levy Gallery, New York.

42. The Bathers—I, 1935. Gouache, 26¾ x 19″.
Collection Mrs. Francis Robbins, Jr., New
York.

43. The Fish Bowl, 1938. Gouache,
21¼ x 17⅝″. Collection Mrs. Le Ray
Berdeau, New York.

44. The Madhouse, 1935. Gouache, 19¼ x 24⅞″. The Museum of Modern Art, New York, Purchase Fund.

45. Pip and Flip, 1935. Oil on canvas, 18 x 15″. Julien Levy Gallery, New York.

46. Leopard Boy, 1935. Oil on canvas, 21⅝ x 18¼". Collection Mr. and Mrs. Henry Clifford, Radnor, Pennsylvania.

47. Portrait of Edith Sitwell, 1937. Oil on canvas. Collection Edward
James, London. *Not included in exhibition.*

48. Portrait of Lincoln Kirstein, 1937. Oil on canvas. Collection Lincoln Kirstein, New York. *Not included in exhibition.*

49. Portrait of Constance Askew, 1938. Oil on canvas, 39 x 39". Collection Mr. and Mrs.
R. Kirk Askew, Jr., New York.

50. Portrait of My Father, 1939. Oil on canvas, 19 x 24⅛". Collection Lincoln Kirstein, New York.

51. Sketch for Phenomena, 1936. Watercolor and ink, 9¾ x 13¾". Private collection.

52. Final Sketch for Phenomena, 1938. Oil on canvas, 35 x 45½". Julien Levy Gallery, New York.

74

53. Phenomena, 1936–38. Oil on canvas, 79 x 106½″. Collection the artist.

54. Leaf Children, 1939. Ink wash, 10¾ x 8⅛″. Collection the artist.

55. Leaf Children, 1939. Gouache, 25¼ x 19¾″. The Museum of Modern Art, New York, Mrs. Simon Guggenheim Fund.

Derby Hill Theme: David and Goliath, 1942. Gouache, 30¼ x 40¼". Collection Miss Agnes Rindge, Poughkeepsie, N. Y.

56. Boys Fighting in Wheat, 1939–41. Oil on canvas, 28⅝ x 18⅛". Collection Dr. A. L. Garbat, New York.

57. The Green Lion, 1942. Gouache, 40 x 30". Collection the artist.

58. Tree in Sussex, 1934. Brown ink, 12 x 15⅝". The Museum of Modern Art, New York, Mrs. Simon Guggenheim Fund.

59. Tree with Children, 1935. Brown ink wash, 12 x 15½". The Museum of Modern Art, New York, Mrs. Simon Guggenheim Fund.

The drawings reproduced on this and the following page partially illustrate the development of Tchelitchew's large composition, *Hide-and-Seek* (plate 68), with particular reference to the evolution of the tree motif from the literal state shown above to its final metamorphic form (plate 61).

60. Tree into Double Hand, 1938–39. Ink wash, 14 x 9¾″. The Museum of Modern Art, New York, Mrs. Simon Guggenheim Fund.

61. Tree into Hand and Foot, 1939. Watercolor and ink, 14 x 9¾″. The Museum of Modern Art, New York, Mrs. Simon Guggenheim Fund.

62. Head of Spring, 1940. Oil on canvas, 20 x 25″. Collection Mr. and Mrs. R. Kirk Askew, Jr., New York.

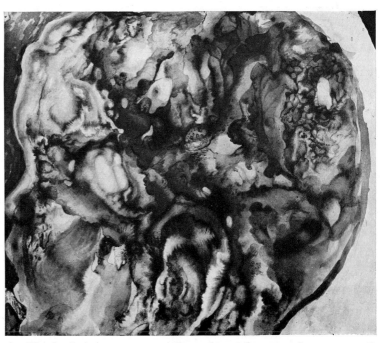

63. Head of Autumn, 1941. Gouache and watercolor, 13 x 15″. Collection Lincoln Kirstein, New York.

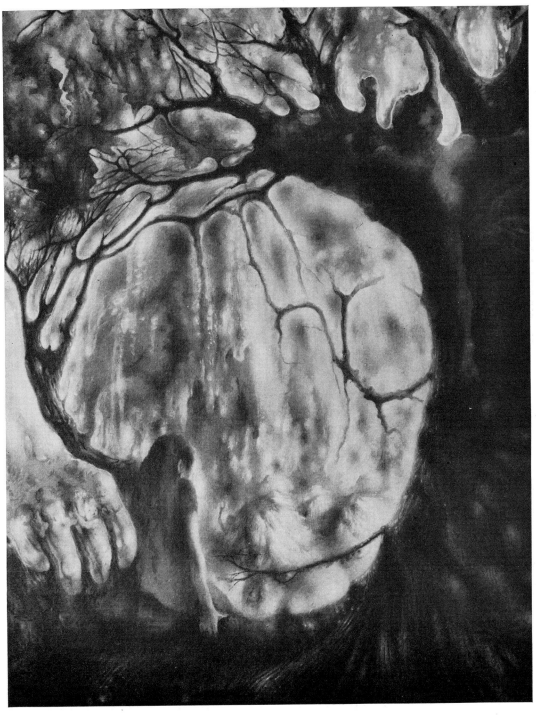

64. Hide-and-Seek, 1940–42. (Detail: "The Drop of Water.") The Museum of Modern Art, New York, Mrs. Simon Guggenheim Fund.

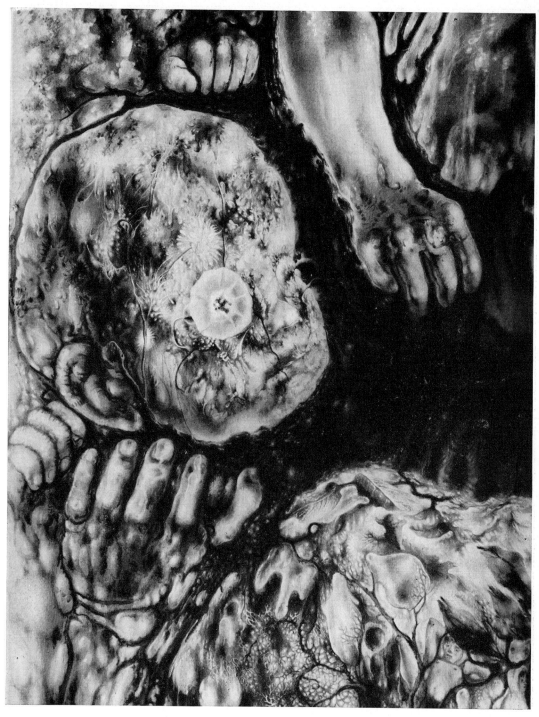

65. Hide-and-Seek, 1940–42. (Detail: "Head of Summer.") The Museum of Modern Art, New York, Mrs. Simon Guggenheim Fund.

66. Hide-and-Seek, 1940–42. (Detail: "Head of Autumn.") The Museum of Modern Art, New York, Mrs. Simon Guggenheim Fund.

67. Sketch for Hide-and-Seek, 1940. Watercolor and ink, 13⅞ x 16¾". Collection the artist.

Hide-and-Seek, 1940–42. Oil on canvas, 78½ x 84¾″. The Museum of Modern Art, New York, Mrs. Simon ɪggenheim Fund.

69. Head of Spahi, 1931. Brown ink wash, 10½ x 8¼". Collection the artist.

70. Musique, 1932. Brown ink wash, 10¼ x 7⅞". Wadsworth Atheneum, Hartford.

88

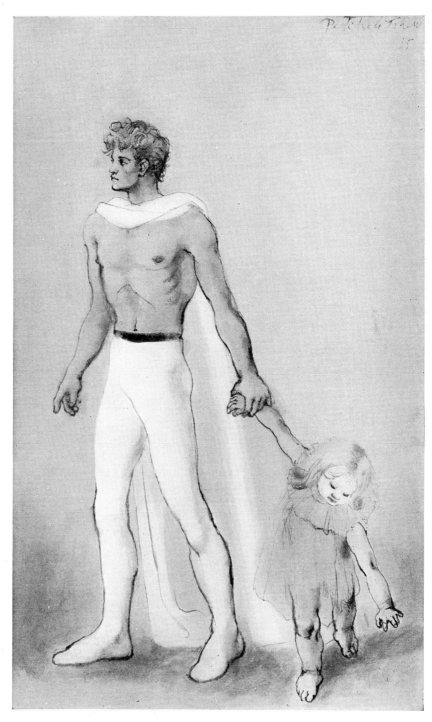

71. Man and Child (*L'Errante*), 1935. Gouache, watercolor and brown ink, 20⅜ x 12¼″. Lifar Collection, Wadsworth Atheneum, Hartford.

72. Metamorphic Landscape, 1941.
Ink wash, 10⅞ x 8½". The Mu-
seum of Modern Art, New York,
Mrs. Simon Guggenheim Fund.

73. The Ogre, 1941. Ink
wash, 13½ x 16¼".
Julien Levy Gallery, New
York.

90

CATALOG AND CHECKLISTS

Paintings

Titles preceded by an asterisk (*) are reproduced in this catalog.

1. HEAD OF A YOUNG MAN, 1925. Oil on canvas, 18 x 15". Collection Mr. and Mrs. Howard Woolf, Scarsdale, N. Y.

* 2. BASKET OF STRAWBERRIES, 1925. Oil on canvas, 15 x 18⅛". Collection Allen Porter, New York.

3. EGGS, 1925. Gouache, 12⅝ x 15". Collection Prof. Ralph W. Church, Santa Barbara, Cal.

* 4. THE SHIP, 1926. Gouache, sand and coffee, 36½ x 28¾". Collection Mr. and Mrs. Sherman Kent, Washington, D.C.

* 5. NUDE, 1926. Oil, sand and coffee on canvas, 39⅛ x 25¼". Collection Julien Levy, New York.

* 6. THE THINKER, 1927. Gouache, sand and coffee, 24¾ x 19". Collection Mr. and Mrs. Sherman Kent, Washington, D.C.

* 7. BLUE ACROBAT, 1927. Gouache, sand and coffee, 24⅞ x 18⅞". Collection Mr. and Mrs. Sherman Kent, Washington, D.C.

* 8. FRUIT, 1927. Gouache and sand, 14¼ x 19¼". Collection Mrs. Charles H. Russell, Jr., New York.

9. STILL LIFE: FLOWERS, 1927. Gouache, 25 x 19¼". Collection Prof. Ralph W. Church, Santa Barbara, Cal.

* 10. CABBAGE, 1928. Gouache and sand, 19⅝ x 25⅝". Collection Miss Margaret C. Prall, Berkeley, Cal.

11. PORTRAIT OF MRS. SHERMAN KENT, 1928 (?). Gouache, sand and coffee on canvas, 31⅞ x 17½". Collection Mr. and Mrs. Sherman Kent, Washington, D.C.

* 12. PORTRAIT OF DAVID PRALL, 1928. Oil and coffee on canvas, 25½ x 19¾". Collection Miss Margaret C. Prall, Berkeley, Cal.

13. PORTRAIT OF MRS. SHERMAN KENT, 1928. Oil on canvas, 32 x 24". Collection Prof. Ralph W. Church, Santa Barbara, Cal.

14. STILL LIFE WITH PEARS, 1928 (?). Oil on canvas, 25 x 20½". Collection Mme. Helena Rubinstein, New York.

* 15. BLUE CLOWN, 1929. Oil on canvas, 31¾ x 23⅝". Private collection.

* 16. CLOWN, 1929. Oil on canvas, 29 x 17½". Collection Mr. and Mrs. Sherman Kent, Washington, D.C.

17. SLEEPING CLOWN, 1929. Oil on canvas, 19¾ x 24". Collection Bernard Davis, Philadelphia.

18. APPLES ON A MANTELPIECE, 1929–30. Oil on canvas, 25⅝ x 21¼". Julien Levy Gallery, New York.

19. HEAD OF A CLOWN, 1929–30. Gouache, 18½ x 12½". Collection James Johnson Sweeney, New York.

* 20. CLOWN RESTING, 1930. Gouache, 15¾ x 31¼". Collection Maurice J. Speiser, New York.

* 21. BURIAL OF THE ACROBAT, 1930. Oil on canvas, 25⅝ x 31⅞". Private collection.

* 22. FALLEN RIDER, 1930. Oil on canvas, 21¼ x 28¾". Collection Bernard Davis, Philadelphia.

* 23. PLASTER HAND, 1930. Oil on canvas, 32 x 23¾". Julien Levy Gallery, New York.

* 24. STILL-LIFE CLOWN, 1930. Oil on canvas, 39⅜ x 25⅝". Private collection.

* 25. SPANISH DANCER, 1930. Oil on canvas, 38 x 28½". Julien Levy Gallery, New York.

26. PORTRAIT OF MME. JEAN BONJEAN, 1930. Oil on canvas, 28¾ x 19½". Museum of Fine Arts, Boston.

* 27. SEATED SPAHI, 1931. Oil on canvas, 36¼ x 28¾". Julien Levy Gallery, New York.

* 28. SLEEPING SPAHI, 1931. Gouache, 29⅜ x 40⅝". Private collection.

* 29. MADAME BONJEAN, 1931. Oil on canvas, 51¼ x 38¼". Private collection.

* 30. THEATRE FRANÇAIS, 1931. Oil on canvas, 29½ x 40". Collection Mr. and Mrs. John E. Abbott, New York.

* 31. NATALIE PALEY AS OPHELIA, 1932. Oil on canvas, 32 x 23¾". Collection Mr. and Mrs. John C. Wilson, New York.

32. PORTRAIT OF MRS. JOHN C. WILSON, 1932. Oil on canvas, 30⅞ x 20⅜". Collection Miss Helen Resor, New York.

33. ANEMONES, 1932. Oil on canvas, 21¾ x 18⅜". Collection Miss Lucy Martin Donnelly, Bryn Mawr, Pa.

* 34. THREE SITTING TOGETHER, 1933. Oil on beaverboard, 29⅝ x 41½". Collection the artist.

* 35. PORTRAIT OF CHARLES HENRI FORD, 1933. Oil on canvas, 39⅝ x 28⅞". Collection Charles Henri Ford, New York.

36. THE TENNIS PLAYERS, 1934. Gouache, 19⅜ x 25⅜". Collection the artist.

* 37. BULLFIGHT, 1934. Gouache, 41½ x 29⅝". Julien Levy Gallery, New York.

* 38. PORTRAIT OF HELENA RUBINSTEIN, 1934. Gouache with sequins, 25 x 20". Collection Mme. Helena Rubinstein, New York.

39. THE MASK OF LIGHT, 1934. Gouache, 25 x 16⅛". Collection Dr. Robert H. Alexander, New York.

40. THE TOREADOR, 1935. Gouache, 24 x 19". Collection Mme. Helena Rubinstein, New York.

* 41. THE BATHERS–I, 1935. Gouache, 26¾ x 19". Collection Mrs. Francis Robbins, Jr., New York.

42. THE BATHERS–II, 1935. Gouache, 30½ x 21". Collection the artist.

* 43. THE MADHOUSE, 1935. Gouache, 19¼ x 24⅞". The Museum of Modern Art, New York, Purchase Fund.

44. THE LORELEI, 1935. Gouache, 18⅞ x 27". Collection Raimund von Hofmannstahl, New York.

* 45. PIP AND FLIP, 1935. Oil on canvas, 18 x 15". Julien Levy Gallery, New York.

* 46. LEOPARD BOY, 1935. Oil on canvas, 21⅝ x 18¼". Collection Mr. and Mrs. Henry Clifford, Radnor, Pa.

47. JERROLD, 1935. Gouache, 17½ x 13¼". Collection Julien Levy, New York.

48. SKETCH FOR PHENOMENA, 1936. Gouache, 17¼ x 23⅝". Collection the artist.

49. THE KITE, 1936. Oil on canvas, 21½ x 14⅞". Julien Levy Gallery, New York.

50. PORTRAIT OF JOELLA, 1937. Gouache, 23⅜ x 19⅜". Collection Miss Agnes Rindge, Poughkeepsie, N. Y.

* 51. PORTRAIT OF CONSTANCE ASKEW, 1938. Oil on canvas, 39 x 39". Collection Mr. and Mrs. R. Kirk Askew, Jr., New York.

* 52. THE FISH BOWL, 1938. Gouache, 21¼ x 17⅝". Collection Mrs. Le Ray Berdeau, New York.

* 53. FINAL SKETCH FOR PHENOMENA, 1938. Oil on canvas, 35 x 45½". Julien Levy Gallery, New York.

* 54. PHENOMENA, 1936–38. Oil on canvas, 79 x 106½". Collection the artist.

55. THE NAP, 1939. Gouache, 19¼ x 25⅛". Collection Edward James, South Laguna, Cal.

56. STUDY FOR BOYS FIGHTING IN WHEAT, 1939. Gouache, 16¾ x 10¾". Collection Dr. Robert H. Alexander, New York.

* 57. BOYS FIGHTING IN WHEAT, 1939–41. Oil on canvas, 28⅜ x 18⅛". Collection Dr. A. L. Garbat, New York.

* 58. PORTRAIT OF MY FATHER, 1939. Oil on canvas, 19 x 24⅛". Collection Lincoln Kirstein, New York.

59. CHILDREN FIGHTING AMONG SUMMER FLOWERS, 1939. Oil on canvas, 25⅝ x 21⅜". Collection Edward James, South Laguna, Cal.

60. THE POPPIES, 1939. Oil on canvas, 24⅞ x 19⅛". Collection Lieut. Stanley R. Resor, New York.

* 61. LEAF CHILDREN, 1939. Gouache, 25¼ x 19¾". The Museum of Modern Art, New York, Mrs. Simon Guggenheim Fund.

62. CHILDREN FIGHTING, 1939. Oil on canvas, 29 x 23½". Collection Edward James, South Laguna, Cal.

63. BLINDFOLDED GIRL, 1939. Gouache, 25¾ x 19¾". Julien Levy Gallery, New York.

64. BOYS IN RUINS, 1939. Gouache, 19¾ x 25½". Collection Edward James, South Laguna, Cal.

65. LITTLE RED RIDING HOOD, 1940. Gouache, 30 x 20". Julien Levy Gallery, New York.

66. THE FLIGHT, 1940. Oil on canvas, 16⅜ x 14¼". Private collection.

67. DERBY HILL THEME: HIAWATHA, 1940. Oil on beaverboard, 28⅞ x 36". Julien Levy Gallery, New York.

* 68. HEAD OF SPRING, 1940. Oil on canvas, 20 x 25". Collection Mr. and Mrs. R. Kirk Askew, Jr., New York.

69. THE ANGEL OF REGRETS, 1941. Oil on board, 24 x 20". Collection the artist.

70. THE CHILDHOOD OF ORSON, 1941. Oil on canvas, 28¼ x 23¼". Collection the artist.

* 71. THE GREEN LION, 1942. Gouache, 40 x 30". Collection the artist.

72. DERBY HILL THEME, 1942. Gouache, 30¼ x 40¼". Collection the artist.

* 73. DERBY HILL THEME: DAVID AND GOLIATH, 1942. Gouache, 30¼ x 40¼". Collection Miss Agnes Rindge, Poughkeepsie, N. Y.

74. DERBY HILL THEME: NIOBE, 1942. Gouache, 30¼ x 40¼". Collection the artist.

75. THE DROP OF WATER, 1942. Oil on canvas, 24 x 20". Private collection.

* 76. HIDE-AND-SEEK, 1940–42. Oil on canvas, 78½ x 84¾". The Museum of Modern Art, New York, Mrs. Simon Guggenheim Fund.

77. PORTRAIT OF BEATRICE GUINLE, 1942. Oil on canvas, 24 x 20". Collection the artist.

Drawings and Studies in Various Media

* 78. ASYMMETRICAL HEAD, 1925 (cover for bibl. 34). Ink, 9 x 12⅛". Collection George Platt Lynes, New York.

79. MULTIPLE NUDE, 1925. Ink, 16⅝ x 9⅝". Collection James Johnson Sweeney, New York.

80. MULTIPLE FIGURES, 1926. Ink, 9 x 4⅝". Collection Miss Margaret C. Prall, Berkeley, Cal.

81. BOY WITH MASK, 1926. Ink, 11½ x 9". Julien Levy Gallery, New York.

* 82. LACONIC COMPOSITION, 1926. Ink, 13⅞ x 9½". Julien Levy Gallery, New York.

83. MULTIPLE FIGURE OF BOY, 1927. Ink, 10⅝ x 9". Julien Levy Gallery, New York.

84. SERGE LIFAR IN "GISELLE," 1928. Brown ink, 17 x 13⅝". Lifar Collection, Wadsworth Atheneum, Hartford.

85. SERGE LIFAR, 1928. Watercolor, 21¾ x 17". Lifar Collection, Wadsworth Atheneum, Hartford.

86. APPLES AND PEARS, 1928. Pencil, 8¼ x 10¾". Collection the artist.

87. FIGURE WITH TRAPEZE, 1928. Ink, 17⅛ x 10⅜". Julien Levy Gallery, New York.

88. STUDY FOR THE HARVESTER, 1928. Gouache, 19 x 12". Collection Mr. and Mrs. R. Kirk Askew, Jr., New York.

* 89. STUDY FOR THE BLUE CLOWN, 1929. Ink wash, 16 x 10½". The Museum of Modern Art, New York, Mrs. Simon Guggenheim Fund.

90. CLOWN, 1929. Ink, 16⅞ x 10⅞". Julien Levy Gallery, New York.

91. CLOWN, 1929. Ink, 18½ x 12½". Collection James Johnson Sweeney, New York.

92. EDITH SITWELL, 1929. Brown ink, 8 x 5½". Collection Mr. and Mrs. John La Touche, New York.

93. CLOWN, 1929. Gouache and watercolor, 21 x 11". Collection Mr. and Mrs. Paul W. Cooley, West Hartford, Conn.

* 94. STUDY AFTER THE CLOWN RESTING, 1930. Brown ink wash, 8½ x 16½". Julien Levy Gallery, New York.

95. THE TRAPEZE, 1930. Brown ink, 17¼ x 12⅜". Julien Levy Gallery, New York.

96. ASLEEP, 1930. Brown ink, 7⅝ x 10⅝". Collection Mr. and Mrs. Paul W. Cooley, West Hartford, Conn.

97. BOY'S HEAD, 1930. Ink, 9⅞ x 7⅜". Julien Levy Gallery, New York.

98. GERTRUDE STEIN, 1930. Ink wash, 14½ x 10¼". Collection Mrs. Charles B. Goodspeed, Chicago.

99. STUDY FOR PENELOPE, 1930. Brown ink, 16¾ x 10¾". Julien Levy Gallery, New York.

100. THE SPAHI, 1930–31. Ink, 13¾ x 10¼". Collection Mr. and Mrs. Russell Lynes, Bryn Mawr, Pa.

*101. HEAD OF SPAHI, 1931. Brown ink wash, 10½ x 8¼". Collection the artist.

102. ACROBAT DISROBING, 1931. Brown ink, 10¼ x 7¾". Private collection.

103. BOY WITH MORNING GLORIES, 1931. Brown ink, 13⅞ x 9⅞". Julien Levy Gallery, New York.

104. BOY WITH ANEMONES, 1931. Ink, 10½ x 8". Collection Mr. and Mrs. R. Kirk Askew, Jr., New York.

105. GERTRUDE STEIN, 1931. Brown ink, 16½ x 10⅛". Collection the artist.

106. FIGURES, 1931. Ink wash, 10¼ x 8". Collection Mrs. Thomas Hart Fisher, Chicago.

107. FIGURES, 1931. Ink wash, 10¼ x 8". Collection Mrs. Thomas Hart Fisher, Chicago.

108. FIGURE, 1930–32 (?). Brown ink, 11 x 8½". Collection Mrs. Joseph Louchheim, Washington, D.C.

109. FIGURE IN ARMOR, 1932. Brown ink wash, 10 3/16 x 7⅞". Collection George Platt Lynes, New York.

110. LEO, 1932 (illustration for bibl. 40). Ink wash, 9 x 12". Collection Monroe Wheeler, New York.

111. BOY WITH STRAW HAT, 1932. Brown ink, 10⅞ x 10¾". Collection Miss Agnes Rindge, Poughkeepsie, N. Y.

112. CIRCASSIAN LADY, 1932. Brown ink, 8½ x 10¾". Collection Miss Agnes Rindge, Poughkeepsie, N. Y.

113. FIGURES IN THE CLOUDS, 1932. Brown ink wash, 10¼ x 14⅛". Julien Levy Gallery, New York.

114. HEAD OF NEGRO SOLDIER, 1932. Ink wash, 10½ x 8". Collection the artist.

*115. MUSIQUE, 1932. Brown ink wash, 10¼ x 7⅞". Wadsworth Atheneum, Hartford.

116. BABY TENNIS PLAYER, 1934. Brown ink, 12¾ x 9¾". Julien Levy Gallery, New York.

117. STUDY FOR PETER THE GREAT, 1934. Brown ink wash, 9¾ x 13". Collection the artist.

118. STUDY FOR THE TENNIS PLAYERS, 1934. Brown ink, 12½ x 9½". Collection the artist.

*119. TREE IN SUSSEX, 1934. Brown ink, 12 x 15⅝". The Museum of Modern Art, New York, Mrs. Simon Guggenheim Fund.

120. CHILD PLAYING HIDE-AND-SEEK, 1934. Brown ink wash, 11½ x 7½". Collection Mrs. Charles B. Goodspeed, Chicago.

*121. TREE WITH CHILDREN, 1935. Brown ink wash, 12 x 15½". The Museum of Modern Art, New York, Mrs. Simon Guggenheim Fund.

122. SPANISH STREET, 1935. Ink, 12¾ x 16". Collection Mr. and Mrs. John C. Wilson, New York.

123. SPANISH SCENE, 1935. Watercolor, 10¾ x 12½". Collection Mme. Helena Rubinstein, New York.

124. FIGURES IN LANDSCAPE, 1935. Ink wash, 12⅝ x 16". Collection Mrs. Charles B. Goodspeed, Chicago.

125. GEORGE PLATT LYNES, 1935. Ink, 15 13/16 x 10 11/16". Collection George Platt Lynes, New York.

126. BEGGARS' LANE, 1935. Ink wash, 26¼ x 26". Collection Leon Kochnitsky, New York.

127. SKETCH FOR PHENOMENA, 1935. Brown ink, 12½ x 16". Collection Lincoln Kirstein, New York.

128. STUDY FOR THE BATHERS–II, 1935. Ink and gouache, 13½ x 9½". Collection Mr. and Mrs. John C. Wilson, New York.

129. FIGURE, 1935. Ink, 13 x 8". Collection the artist.

130. SKETCH FOR THE FISH BOWL, 1935. Ink, 16 x 10¾". Collection the artist.

*131. SKETCH FOR PHENOMENA, 1936. Watercolor and ink, 9¾ x 13¾". Private collection.

132. SKETCH FOR PHENOMENA, 1936. Ink wash, 13 x 19¼". Collection the artist.

133. PORTRAIT, 1937. Silverpoint, 18⅞ x 12⅝". Collection Mrs. Oliver B. Jennings, New York.

134. FIGURES, 1937. Ink, 14 x 16⅞". Collection the artist.

135. PARKER TYLER, 1937. Silverpoint, 17½ x 11⅝". Collection the artist.

136. FIGURES AT ISCHIA, 1937. Ink, 13⅝ x 16½". Collection the artist.

137. PETER, 1937. Watercolor, 13⅝ x 9". Collection Mrs. Josiah P. Marvel, Princeton, N.J.

138. THE WAIFS, 1937 (?). Silverpoint, 17 x 12". Collection Lincoln Kirstein, New York.

139. NUDE, 1937. Ink and gouache, 13 x 8⅝". Collection Lincoln Kirstein, New York.

140. FIGURES, 1937. Pencil, 16½ x 13⅜". Collection the artist.

141. ABE, 1937. Silverpoint, 16⅞ x 10⅞". Collection the artist.

142. NUDE, 1937. Silverpoint, 19⅜ x 12⅝". Collection Miss Edith Wetmore, New York.

143. SCENE AT ISCHIA, 1937. Ink, 13⅜ x 16⅜". Collection Wright Ludington, Santa Barbara, Cal.

144. FIGURES AT ISCHIA, 1937. Ink, 13⅜ x 16⅜". Collection Wright Ludington, Santa Barbara, Cal.

145. FIGURES, 1937. Brown ink, 16½ x 13½". Collection the artist.

146. FREDERICK ASHTON, 1938. Silverpoint, 18 x 12⅛". Collection the artist.

147. BOYS WITH SAILBOAT, 1938. Ink wash, 13⅝ x 9 11/16". Collection Monroe Wheeler, New York.

148. HEAD OF WOMAN, 1938. Colored ink and watercolor, 18⅝ x 12". Collection Edgar Kaufmann, Pittsburgh.

149. GIRL RUNNING, 1938. Colored ink, 14 x 9¾". Collection the artist.

150. WOMAN AND CHILD, 1938. Silverpoint, 12¼ x 15¾". Collection the artist.

151. PORTRAIT OF NICHOLAS KOPEIKINE, 1938 (?). Silverpoint, 19 x 12¾" Collection Dr. Burrill B. Crohn, New York.

152. SKETCH FOR PHENOMENA, 1938. Brown ink, 15 x 13½". Collection the artist.

*153. TREE INTO DOUBLE HAND, 1938–39. Ink wash, 14 x 9¾". The Museum of Modern Art, New York, Mrs. Simon Guggenheim Fund.

*154. TREE INTO HAND AND FOOT, 1939. Watercolor and ink, 14 x 9¾". The Museum of Modern Art, New York, Mrs. Simon Guggenheim Fund.

155. TREE INTO HAND AND FOOT WITH CHILDREN, c. 1939. Ink wash, 13⅞ x 16¾". The Museum of Modern Art, New York, Mrs. Simon Guggenheim Fund.

156. THE DANDELION, 1939. Watercolor and gouache, 11 x 8½". The Museum of Modern Art, New York, Mrs. Simon Guggenheim Fund.

157. RECLINING WOMAN AS MOUNTAIN, 1939. Ink, 10½ x 17". Julien Levy Gallery, New York.

158. STUDY FOR PORTRAIT OF MY FATHER, 1939. Gouache, 9½ x 13¼". Julien Levy Gallery, New York.

159. THE PROCESSION, 1939 (?). Watercolor and brown ink, 10½ x 15⅜". Collection Wright Ludington, Santa Barbara, Cal.

160. SKETCH FOR FATA MORGANA, 1939. Watercolor, 13½ x 16½". Collection Mr. and Mrs. John E. Abbott, New York.

161. LEAVES, 1939. Pencil, 10⅝ x 8¼". Collection the artist.

162. FIRST STUDY FOR THE DROP OF WATER, 1939. Ink wash, 15 x 10¾". Collection the artist.

163. LEAF CHILDREN, 1939. Ink and gouache, 14 x 10". Collection the artist.

164. FIGURES ON CLOTHESLINE, 1939. Ink wash, 11 x 8¼". Collection the artist.

165. LEAF CHILDREN, 1939. Ink wash, 11 x 8¼". Collection the artist.

166. FLOWER CHILDREN, 1939. Ink wash, 17¼ x 10¾". Collection the artist.

*167. LEAF CHILDREN, 1939. Ink wash, 10¾ x 8⅛". Collection the artist.

168. TWO STUDIES OF AUTUMN LEAVES, 1939. Ink and gouache, 10½ x 8¼". Collection the artist.

169. PINK LEAVES, 1939. Colored ink and gouache, 16¾ x 13¾". Collection the artist.

170. STUDY FOR PORTRAIT OF HELEN RESOR, 1940 (?). Gouache and water color, 17½ x 11⅛". Collection Lieut. Stanley R. Resor, New York.

171. MRS. JOHN C. WILSON, 1940. Silverpoint, 14¾ x 11⅜". Collection Mr. and Mrs. John C. Wilson, New York.

172. HEAD OF SPRING, 1940. Ink wash, 8½ x 11". Collection the artist.

173. HEAD OF SPRING, 1940. Gouache, watercolor and ink, 15 x 20". Collection the artist.

174. HEAD OF SPRING, 1940. Gouache, watercolor and ink, 15 x 20". Collection the artist.

175. THE DROP OF WATER, 1940. Ink wash, 8½ x 11". Collection the artist.

176. THE DROP OF WATER, 1940. Gouache, watercolor and ink, 14¾ x 20". Collection the artist.

*177. SKETCH FOR HIDE-AND-SEEK, 1940. Watercolor and ink, 13⅞ x 16¾". Collection the artist.

178. HEAD OF AUTUMN, 1941. Ink wash, 12½ x 14⅝". The Museum of Modern Art, New York, Mrs. Simon Guggenheim Fund.

179. HEAD OF AUTUMN, 1941. Ink wash, 10⅞ x 8⅜". Collection the artist.

180. HEAD OF AUTUMN, 1941. Gouache, watercolor and ink, 13¾ x 16¾". Collection the artist.

181. HEAD OF AUTUMN, 1941. Gouache, watercolor and ink, 9½ x 11". Collection the artist.

*182. HEAD OF AUTUMN, 1941. Gouache and watercolor, 13 x 15". Collection Lincoln Kirstein, New York.

183. HEAD OF SUMMER, 1941. Watercolor, 15 x 11". Collection the artist.

*184. THE OGRE, 1941. Ink wash, 13½ x 16¼". Julien Levy Gallery, New York.

185. ALEXANDER BULL, 1941. Pencil, 15¾ x 12". Collection Harry A. Bull, New York.

186. METAMORPHIC LANDSCAPE, 1941. Ink wash, 10⅜ x 8". Julien Levy Gallery, New York.

187. METAMORPHOSIS WITH CHILDREN AND CATS, 1941. Ink, 10¾ x 8¼". Julien Levy Gallery, New York.

188. METAMORPHOSIS, 1941. Watercolor, 9⅜ x 11⅞". Julien Levy Gallery, New York.

189. METAMORPHIC LANDSCAPE WITH NIGHT-HAWK, 1941. Ink wash, 10¾ x 13½". Collection Monroe Wheeler, New York.

*190. METAMORPHIC LANDSCAPE, 1941. Ink wash, 10⅞ x 8½". The Museum of Modern Art, New York, Mrs. Simon Guggenheim Fund.

191. THE EAR, 1941. Ink wash, 10⅞ x 8⅜". Collection the artist.

192. PORTRAIT OF MRS. E. GERRY CHADWICK, 1942. Gouache, watercolor and ink, 18 x 12⅞". Collection Mrs. E. Gerry Chadwick, New York.

193. BRANCH ANATOMY, 1942. Ink wash, 17¼ x 11¾". Collection the artist.

Ballet and Theatre Designs 1928–41

ODE, 1928.

Ballet in one act. Book: Boris Kochno. Music: Nicolas Nabokov. Choreography: Léonide Massine. Scenery and costumes: Pavel Tchelitchew. Presented by Serge de Diaghilev at the *Théâtre Sarah Bernhardt*, Paris, June 6, 1928.

194. Design for Program Cover. Gouache and ink, 14 x 9". Lifar Collection, Wadsworth Atheneum, Hartford.

195. Study of Dancers. Ink wash, 18¼ x 11⅞". Lifar Collection, Wadsworth Atheneum, Hartford.

196. Costume Design. Gouache, watercolor and ink, 12⅜ x 9⅜". Lifar Collection, Wadsworth Atheneum, Hartford.

197. Costume Design. Gouache, watercolor and ink, 12¼ x 9⅜". Lifar Collection, Wadsworth Atheneum, Hartford.

L'ERRANTE, 1933.

Ballet in one act of one scene. Book: Pavel Tchelitchew and George Balanchine. Music: Schubert, orchestrated by Charles Koechlin. Choreography: George Balanchine. Scenery and costumes: Pavel Tchelitchew. Presented by "Les Ballets 1933" at the *Théâtre des Champs Elysées*, Paris, June 10, 1933. Revived by the American Ballet Company at the Adelphi Theatre, New York, March 11, 1935.

198. Four Dancers, 1935. Gouache, watercolor and brown ink, 9½ x 19¾". Lifar Collection, Wadsworth Atheneum, Hartford.

199. Two Dancers in Green, 1935. Gouache, watercolor and brown ink, 10½ x 16½". Lifar Collection, Wadsworth Atheneum, Hartford.

200. Three Dancers in Red, 1935. Gouache, watercolor and brown ink, 12½ x 19½". Lifar Collection, Wadsworth Atheneum, Hartford.

201. Two Angels, 1935. Gouache and brown ink, 17⅜ x 8⅜". Lifar Collection, Wadsworth Atheneum, Hartford.

202. Two Male Dancers, 1935. Gouache, watercolor and brown ink, 19¼ x 12¼". Lifar Collection, Wadsworth Atheneum, Hartford.

*203. Man and Child, 1935. Gouache, watercolor and brown ink, 20⅜ x 12¼". Lifar Collection, Wadsworth Atheneum, Hartford.

MAGIC, 1936.

Ballet-serenata in one scene. Music: Mozart. Choreography: George Balanchine. Scenery and costumes: Pavel Tchelitchew. Presented by Felia Doubrowska and dancers of the American Ballet Company at the Avery Memorial Auditorium, The Wadsworth Atheneum, Hartford, February 14, 1936.

204. Dancer with Candelabra. Watercolor and ink, 15⅞ x 9¾". Wadsworth Atheneum, Hartford.

205. Musician. Watercolor and ink, 9⅞ x 6⅞". Wadsworth Atheneum, Hartford.

206. Sorceress. Watercolor and ink, 15¾ x 9¾". Wadsworth Atheneum, Hartford.

207. Décor. Watercolor and ink, 9 x 13⅝". Wadsworth Atheneum, Hartford.

ORPHEUS, 1936.

Opera-ballet in two acts, four scenes. Book: Ranieri Calzabigi. Music: Christoph Willibald von Gluck. Choreography: George Balanchine. Scenery and costumes: Pavel Tchelitchew. Presented by the American Ballet Company at the Metropolitan Opera House, New York, May 22, 1936.

208. 4 Costume Designs. Gouache, 17½ x 8½" (average). The Museum of Modern Art, New York, Dance Archives.

NOBILISSIMA VISIONE or SAINT FRANCIS, 1938.

Ballet in one act of five scenes. Book: Paul Hindemith and Léonide Massine. Music: Paul Hindemith. Choreography: Léonide Massine. Scenery and costumes: Pavel Tchelitchew. Presented by the Ballet Russe de Monte Carlo at the Drury Lane Theatre, London, July 21, 1938.

209. 4 Costume Designs. Gouache, each 20⅜ x 9¾". The Museum of Modern Art, New York, Dance Archives.

ONDINE, 1939.

Play in three acts. Author: Jean Giraudoux. Director: Louis Jouvet. Scenery and costumes: Pavel Tchelitchew. Produced by Louis Jouvet at the *Théâtre de l'Athenée*, Paris, June 1, 1939.

210. Décor. Watercolor, 12¾ x 17⅜". Julien Levy Gallery, New York.

BALUSTRADE, 1941.

Ballet in one act (four movements). Music: Igor Stravinsky. Choreography: George Balanchine. Scenery and costumes: Pavel Tchelitchew. Presented by W. de Basil's Original Ballet Russe at the 51st Street Theatre, New York, January 22, 1941.

211. Costume Design. Watercolor, 13¼ x 10½". Collection A. Everett Austin, Jr., Hartford.

212. Costume Design. Gouache, 13 x 10¾". Collection Lincoln Kirstein, New York.

213. Costume Design. Ink, 11 x 8½". Collection Mrs. Oliver B. Jennings, New York.

THE CAVE OF SLEEP, 1941.

Ballet in one act of five scenes. Book: Pavel Tchelitchew. Music: Paul Hindemith. Choreography: George Balanchine. Scenery and costumes: Pavel Tchelitchew. Commissioned by Lincoln Kirstein and George Balanchine, April, 1941. (Unproduced.)

214. Costume Design. Gouache, 16 x 8⅝". The Museum of Modern Art, New York, Dance Archives.

215. 3 Costume Designs. Gouache, each 14 x 11". The Museum of Modern Art, New York, Dance Archives.

216. 3 Costume Designs. Gouache, each 14 x 11". The Museum of Modern Art, New York, Dance Archives.

Exhibitions of Tchelitchew's Works.

Bibl. refers to numbered entry in the bibliography.

1924(?) PARIS. Galerie Henry (Summer). Drawings in pencil and color. [With works by Bart, Lanskoy, Terechkovitch.] Data supplied by the artist.

1924(?) LONDON. Redfern Gallery (June-July). Drawings. [With works by Joseph Lubitsch.] Data supplied by the artist.

1925 PARIS. Salon d'Automne. [Exhibited the *Basket of Strawberries* and *Portrait of Claudia Pavlova.*]

1926 PARIS. Galerie Druet (Feb. 22-Mar. 5). [With Christian Bérard, Eugène Berman, Léonide Berman, Pierre Charbonnier, Thérèse Debains, J.-F. Laglenne, L. de Angelis and K. Tonny.]
Comment by Stein, bibl. 33.

1928 LONDON. Claridge Gallery (July). Paintings, gouaches, watercolors.
Comment by Sitwell, bibl. 31.

1929 PARIS. Galerie Pierre (June). Paintings.

1930 NEW YORK. Museum of Modern Art (Apr. 12-26). 46 painters and sculptors under 35 years of age. [Included 4 Tchelitchew paintings.]

1931 HARTFORD, CONN. Wadsworth Atheneum (Apr. 15-May 7). [With Bérard, Berman, Léonide, Tonny.]
Catalog, bibl. 18.

1931 NEW YORK. Balzac Galleries (Mar. 21-Apr. 9). Paintings, watercolors, drawings by Tchelitchew, Berman, Léonide, Bérard. [Included 9 works by Tchelitchew.]

1931 PARIS. Galerie Vignon (June 2-15). Paintings, pastels, gouaches.

1932 PARIS. Galerie Vignon (Feb.). Drawings. [With Bérard, Berman, Léonide, Tonny, Lubitsch and Alexander Calder.]

1932 THE HAGUE. Esther Surrey Gallery. Date cited by Waldemar George (bibl. 13), corroborated by artist.

1932 POUGHKEEPSIE, N. Y. Vassar College (Nov. 6-Dec. 4). Paintings and drawings by Eugène Berman and Pavlik Tchelitchew.

1933 ANTWERP. Salon d'Art Contemporain (June).

1933 HARTFORD, CONN. Wadsworth Atheneum (Jan. 24-Feb. 14). Literature and poetry in painting since 1850. [Nos. 71-72 by Tchelitchew.]
Catalog, bibl. 19.

1933 LONDON. Arthur Tooth & Sons Ltd. (Feb. 23-Mar. 18). Paintings.

1933 NEW YORK. Julien Levy Gallery (Feb. 24/25-Mar. 18). Drawings.

1934 NEW YORK. Julien Levy Gallery (Dec. 12-31). Drawings and paintings.
Catalog, bibl. 26.

1935 CHICAGO. Arts Club (Jan.). Paintings and drawings.

1935 LONDON. Arthur Tooth & Sons Ltd. (Oct. 24-Nov. 16). Paintings, gouaches, drawings.

1937 NEW YORK. Julien Levy Gallery (Nov. 2-22). Portraits [paintings, drawings, sketches, silverpoints].

1937 NORTHAMPTON, MASS. Smith College (Nov. 30-Dec. 18). Portraits.

1938 CHICAGO. Arts Club (Feb.). Portraits and drawings.

1938 LONDON. Arthur Tooth & Sons Ltd. (June 16-July 9). *Phenomena* [also gouaches, pastels and drawings].
Catalog, bibl. 25.

1938 NEW YORK. Julien Levy Gallery (Oct. 25-Nov. 15). *Phenomena.*

1939 PARIS. Galerie de Quatre Chemins (Apr.). Fifteen years of drawing.

1939 PARIS. Chez René Drouin (May 16-30). *Phenomena.*

1940 NEW YORK. Julien Levy Gallery (Jan. 23-Feb. 23). A Decade of painting, 1929–1939. [Nos. 79-88 by Tchelitchew.]
Gallery stock show.

1940 NEW YORK. Julien Levy Gallery (Apr. 20-May 7). Drawings, 1925–1940.

1940 NEW YORK. Steuben Glass, Inc. (Jan. 10-Mar. 2). Designs in glass by twenty-seven contemporary artists. [No. 25 by Tchelitchew.]
Catalog, bibl. 36.

1940 PARIS. Galerie des Quatre Chemins (Mar.). Watercolors.

1941 SAN FRANCISCO. Julien Levy Gallery (Sept. 30-Oct. 14). Paintings and drawings by Berman, Tchelitchew, Léonide, Bérard. [Nos. 9-14 by Tchelitchew.]
Exhibited at Courvoisier Galleries in San Francisco.

1942 NEW YORK. Julien Levy Gallery (Apr. 21-May 18). Metamorphoses [drawings, gouaches, paintings, watercolors].

BIBLIOGRAPHY

The arrangement of this bibliography is alphabetical, under the author's name wherever possible. The bibliographical form is modelled upon that used in the Art Index.

ABBREVIATIONS: * in the Museum of Modern Art Library, √ seen by the compiler, † not seen by the compiler, but listed because of its inclusion in a reliable bibliography.

Ap *April*, col il *colored illustration(s)*, cop *copyright*, D *December*, ed *editor(s)*, F *February*, il *illustration(s)*, Ja *January*, Je *June*, Jy *July*, l *leaves*, Mr *March*, My *May*, N *November*, no *number*, n.s. *new series*, O *October*, p *page(s)*, pl *plate(s)*, por *portrait*, S *September*, ser *series*.

SAMPLE ENTRY for magazine article: FROST, ROSAMUND. Tchelitchew: method into magic (Contemporary contour no.16). 6il (por) Art News 41:24-5 Ap 15 1942

EXPLANATION: An article by Rosamund Frost, entitled "Tchelitchew: method into magic," including six illustrations with a portrait, will be found in Art News, volume 41, pages 24-25, April 15, 1942.

* 1. AMERICAN BALLET, primera jira interamericana, junio-diciembre de 1941, bajo los auspicios de la Sociedad Musical Daniel.
> Publicity program. Section on *Escenógrafos* includes portrait and brief notice.

* 2. Artists in exile. col il Fortune 24:103-115 D 1941.
> "Pavel Tchelitchew," p112.

√ 3. BEATON, CECIL. Cecil Beaton's scrapbook. London, B. T. Batsford, 1937.
> "Ode," p125-126.—"L'Errante" (photograph), p95.—Pavel Tchelitchew painting (photograph), p85.

√ 4. —— Cecil Beaton's New York. 261p il Philadelphia and New York, J. B. Lippincott, 1938.
> Pavel Tchelitchew, p235-237.

† 5. BELL, G. Freak show. New Statesman and Nation 15:1063-64 Je 25 1938.

† 6. DER BLAUE VOGEL. 2.heft p8+ il F 1922; 3.heft p5+ il S 1922.

* 7. COTON, A. V. A Prejudice for ballet. 237p il London, Methuen & Co., 1938.
> "Ode . . . Décor, dresses, and staging effects by Tchelitchev and Charbonnier," p85-89.

* 8. CREVEL, RENÉ. L'Esprit contre la raison, édition ornée d'un portrait par Tchelitchew. 56p Marseille, Cahiers du Sud, 1927.

√ 9. FLANNER, JANET. The Spring scene in Paris. [Comment on sales of Tchelitchew at the Tooth Gallery, London] il Arts and Decoration 39:33,62 Je 1933.

*10. [FRIENDS AND ENEMIES OF MODERN MUSIC, INC.] The first Hartford festival 31p il [Hartford, 1936].
> The festival was held in association with the Wadsworth Atheneum. Henry-Russell Hitchcock, jr., edited the program. Designs for the cover, the paper ball and the ballet décors by Pavel Tchelitchew. Portrait by George Platt Lynes, p27.

*11. FROST, ROSAMUND. Tchelitchew: method into magic (Contemporary contour no.16). 6il (por) Art News 41:24-5 Ap 15 1942.

*12. GEORGE, WALDEMAR. Art in Paris: Tchelitcheff. Formes 16:107 Je 1931.

*13. —— Le Néo-humanisme. In R. Huyghe, ed. Histoire de l'art contemporain; la peinture. p359-362 Paris, Alcan, 1935.
> Reprinted from L'Amour de l'Art 15:359-362 Ap 1934 with enlarged bibliography. For abridged edition see 21.

*14. —— 1933 ballets and the spirit of contemporary art. 4il (2 col) Formes 33:377-9 1933.

√15. —— Paul Tchelitchew. 4il Apollo 17:40-2 F 1933.

*16. —— Paul Tchelitchew—towards a humanist art. 4il Formes 9:6-7 N 1930.

√17. GROHMANN, W. Paul Tchelitschew. In Ulrich Thieme & Felix Becker, eds. Allgemeines lexikon der bildenden künstler 32:497 Leipzig, E. A. Seemann, 1938.
> Bibliography.

*18. HARTFORD, CONN. WADSWORTH ATHENEUM. Tonny, Tchelitchew, Bérard, Berman, Léonide. [11]p il 1931.
> Exhibition catalog; "Pavel Tchelitchew," p1-2.

*19. —— An Exhibition of literature & poetry in painting since 1850, January 24-February 14, 1933, The Wadsworth Atheneum and Morgan Memorial, Hartford.
> Exhibition catalog; "Tchelitchew," p21.

√20. —— The President and trustees of the Wadsworth Atheneum, Hartford, Connecticut, invite you to attend a paper ball "Le

Cirque des Chiffoniers" designed by Pavel Tchelitchew on Saturday, February 15th for the benefit of the Wadsworth Atheneum. [2 l] il [1936].

Printed invitation to the first Hartford festival.

*21. HUYGHE, RENÉ. Histoire de l'art contemporain; la peinture. 536p il Paris, Alcan, 1935.

"Les tendances actuelles; introduction," p355-358. Reprinted from L'Amour de l'Art 15:355-358 Ap 1934.

Abridged edition: La peinture française, les contemporains. [84]p plus 160 plates Paris, Pierre Tisné, 1939 "Le Néo-humanisme," p58.

English translation by Paul C. Blum: French painting, the contemporaries. New York, French and European Publications, 1939.

V 22. IMBS, BRAVIG. Confessions of another young man. New York, Henkle-Yewdale House, Inc., 1936 302p.

Memoirs of Paris in the middle '20s with the Gertrude Stein circle which included Tchelitchew, Bérard, Virgil Thomson, Elliot Paul and others.

*23. KIRSTEIN, LINCOLN. The Book of the dance. 388p il Garden City, N. Y., Garden City Publishing Co., 1942 cop 1935.

"Ode of Nicholas Nabokoff, Pavel Tchelitcheff and Léonide Massine (1928)," p301-3, il (no 115).

——— The Position of Tchelitchew.

See 39.

*24. KRAUS, H. FELIX. French moderns in America —[part] II. Studio: 123:165-168 Je 1942.

*25. LONDON. ARTHUR TOOTH & SONS LTD. Phenomena by Pavel Tchelitchew, exhibition June 16-July 9, 1938.

Exhibition catalog; commentary on "Phenomena" p[1].

*26. NEW YORK. JULIEN LEVY GALLERY. Pavel Tchelitchew . . . on exhibition December 12-31 [1934].

Exhibition catalog; quotation by Osbert Sitwell, notice by [Julien Levy].

*27. NEW YORK. MUSEUM OF MODERN ART LIBRARY. [Paul Tchelitchew, miscellaneous uncataloged material].

A folder of catalogs, clippings and reproductions.

V 28. NEW YORK. PUBLIC LIBRARY. ART DIVISION. [Paul Tchelitchew, miscellaneous uncataloged material].

A folder of catalogs, clippings and reproductions.

*29. RAYNAL, MAURICE. Anthologie de la peinture en France de 1906 à nos jours. 320p il Paris, Editions Montaigne, 1927.

Tchelitchew, p291-94; 2il.

English translation by Ralph Roeder: Modern French painters p152-3. New York, Brentano's, 1928.

V 30. REFN, HELGE. Pavel Tchelitchew. 3il p250-1 Samlaren D 1938.

V 31. SITWELL, EDITH. [Miss Edith Sitwell presents a genius?] 4il p133 The Graphic (London) Jy 28 1928.

Eulogy of exhibit at Claridge gallery.

*32. SOBY, JAMES THRALL. After Picasso. Hartford, Edwin Valentine Mitchell; New York, Dodd, Mead & Co., 1935.

The Neo-Romantics, p11-13; Pavel Tchelitchew, p23-31; Illustrations, pl7-12.

——— Return to the north.

See 39.

*33. STEIN, GERTRUDE. The Autobiography of Alice B. Toklas. New York, Harcourt, Brace & Co., 1933.

"The young russian . . ." p277-280.

V 34. ——— Descriptions of literature. Englewood, N. J., As Stable Publications, 1926.

Drawing by Tchelitchew printed on front cover. As Stable Pamphlet II, May 1926, issued by Edith Finch, George Platt Lynes, Adlai Harbeck.

*35. ——— Dix portraits. il (por) Paris, Editions de la Montaigne, 1930.

"Pavlik Tchelitchef or Adrian Arthur," p23-5.

Text in English and French.

*36. STEUBEN GLASS, INC., NEW YORK. The Collection of designs in glass by twenty-seven contemporary artists. [66]p [New York, The firm, 1940].

Illustrated catalog of an exhibition.

Biographical note and illustration, no. 25.

*37. THÉÂTRE DES CHAMPS-ELYSÉES, PARIS. M. Edward James présente Les Ballets 1933 de George Balanchine. 16p il [Paris, 1933].

Souvenir program. "L'Errante, fantasie chorégraphique . . . décor et costumes de Pavel Tchelitchew." p7-9 5il (2 col).

*38. To the dawn of a better décor at the Opera. il Art News 41:9-11,33-34 Mr 15 1942.

TYLER, PARKER. Tchelitchew's world.

See 39.

*39. VIEW. ser 2, no 2 My 1942.

Special issue (13p, 16il) with articles on Tchelitchew by Parker Tyler, James Thrall Soby, Lincoln Kirstein, William Carlos Williams.

*40. WESCOTT, GLENWAY. A Calendar of saints for unbelievers; the text by Glenway Wescott; the signs of the zodiac by Pavel Tchelitchew. 239p il [Paris] Harrison of Paris, 1932.

*41. What the Metropolitan Opera might do: an ideal for the "Magic Flute." il Art News 41:8 Mr 15 1942.
   Commentary by Tchelitchew on his design for "Queen of the Night."

*42. White Russian painter puts his world in 63 square feet of canvas. 2il (por) Life p56-7 S 5 1938.

*43. WILENSKI, REGINALD HOWARD. Modern French painters. 424p New York, Reynal & Hitchcock [1940].
   Tchelitchew, p301,313,314,325; il (facing p307).

WILLIAMS, WILLIAM CARLOS. Cache-cache. See 39.

The artist in his studio, New York, 1942. Photo by George Platt Lynes.

SIX THOUSAND COPIES OF THIS BOOK HAVE BEEN PRINTED AND BOUND IN OCTOBER, 1942, FOR THE TRUSTEES OF THE MUSEUM OF MODERN ART BY THE AMERICAN BOOK–STRATFORD PRESS, NEW YORK. THE COLOR INSERTS WERE PRINTED BY THE SPIRAL PRESS, NEW YORK.